# Knitting Stitches

# Knitting Stitches

Over 300 Contemporary and
Traditional Stitch Patterns

## Mary Webb

FIREFLY BOOKS

# A FIREFLY BOOK

Published by Firefly Books Ltd. 2006

First printing

Publisher Cataloging-in-Publication Data (U.S.)

Knitting stitches : over 300 contemporary and traditional stitch patterns / Webb, Mary
[352] p. : col. ill. col. ;   cm.
Includes index.
Summary: A small-format, portable guide to over 300 stitch patterns.
ISBN-13: 978-1-55407-214-9
ISBN-10: 1-55407-214-X
1. Knitting. I. Webb, Mary. II. Title.
746.43/ 042  dc22   TT820.K55  2006


Library and Archives Canada Cataloguing in Publication

Knitting stitches : over 300 contemporary and traditional stitches / Webb, Mary
Includes index.
ISBN-13: 978-1-55407-214-9
ISBN-10: 1-55407-214-X
1. Knitting.  I. Webb, Mary, 1966-
TT820.K55 2006     746.43'042     C2006-902249-6


Published in the United States by
Firefly Books (U.S.) Inc.
P.O. Box 1338, Ellicott Station
Buffalo, New York 14205

Published in Canada by
Firefly Books Ltd.
66 Leek Crescent
Richmond Hill, Ontario L4B 1H1

Design and layout by e-Digital Design

Manufactured in Singapore by Pica Digital Pte Ltd
Printed in China by L Rex Printing Co Ltd

# Contents

# Introduction

Knitting is the art of constructing a flexible fabric from a notionally continuous thread. The surface of the fabric can be smooth or textured, and the knitted pieces can be flat or tubular, straight or shaped in infinite variety. All you need to know to get started is how to hold the yarn and needles, how to cast on and bind off and the two basic stitches, knit and purl.

The combination of knit and purl stitches ranges from the abstract to the pictorial. Cable offers a highly embossed effect and is probably the most versatile technique there is; it can be used by itself or with other stitch patterns. Bobble and lace stitches are wonderfully complementary, as are twisted stitches.

This book is divided into nine sections – the first three introduce you to materials and basic techniques that you need to have to start to knit. The remaining sections are a library of stitches and patterns divided into Knit and Purl, Rib stitches, Cable stitches, Lace and Bobble stitches and Twist and other stitches. Knit and Purl is probably the simplest technique and Cable the most versatile, usable on its own or with other stitch patterns. Each section is divided into Popular stitches and Patterns followed by Easy, Medium and Difficult stitches.

Charts have been used to explain the stitch patterns because they are more concise and explicit than stitch-by-stitch written instructions, although both are used in the early pages as an aid to readers who are unfamiliar with charted instructions. Learning to work from charts is not difficult if it's taken one step at a time.

A knitter with basic skills will quickly gain confidence as the principles of working from charts are understood. The charts are fully explained in a section at the beginning of the book, followed by a list of abbreviations and a glossary of symbols.

Before selecting a stitch and casting on, it's important to remember that knitting is about creating a fabric as well as making decorative patterns. Some hand-knitted fabrics are more stable than others, some are more dense, some are open, some expand and some contract, so it's essential to consider the use that the knitting will be put to when selecting yarn and stitch.

The majority of designs in the book are easy to follow and a large chart may be based on repetition rather than complexity. So don't be afraid to tackle something just because it's large scale or looks complicated.

Have a go and happy knitting!

# Materials
# & Tools

# Yarn

Selecting yarn is an important decision to make, as it will strongly influence the look of your finished piece.

There are three main characteristics to consider: the yarn's thickness (ply), the fiber content, and the manufacturer's treatment of the fiber. Thick yarns tend to produce bulkier fabrics, while thinner yarns produce finer ones. Fibers can be from animal, plant or synthetic origin, and each fiber has specific properties that will affect the knitted fabric. In addition, the fiber can be treated and spun to make it heavier, denser, twisted, flatter, lighter or hairier. It is the combination of these factors that creates the tactile qualities of yarn, which in turn will determine the texture and character of your knitted article.

### • Wool

The most common yarn used in knitting, wool is a great warm, winter yarn. It is durable and easy to work with, and is good for plain knitting. Its natural elasticity makes it good for rib and cable fabrics that need to pull in and stretch.

It is a versatile fiber and blends well with other yarns. Depending on how it is spun, it can be fine and delicate, or heavier and more rugged. It is often spun with a smooth appearance, which is ideal for showing stitch detail.

### • Mohair

Often classed as a fashion yarn due to its unique hairy fabric surface, mohair can be blended with other fibers to reduce its fluffiness. The types shown are mixed with wool and with silk to give a fine appearance and a refined, luxurious feel.

### • Silk

This is available in two qualities: wild, which produces a coarse thread, and cultivated, which produces a finer thread. As both are expensive, silk is associated with luxury. As a knitting yarn it can be quite brittle; its nonelastic quality makes it unsuitable for clinging or stretchy stitches. For this reason it is often blended with other fibers to make it more versatile.

## • Angora and Cashmere

Both are expensive, but they have a wonderfully soft and luxurious feel. Cashmere can be used in its pure form, but is more widely used blended with another fiber such as silk or wool. Angora is often blended with wool.

## • Cotton

Cotton is made from a natural plant fiber and, although historically used as a summer yarn, is warm in the winter and cool in the summer. It generally has a smooth appearance, and can be crisp or soft depending on how it has been produced.

## • Linen

Linen is made from the stem of the flax plant. It is very strong and washes well. It absorbs moisture so is often good in hot climates. Linen can be stiff and has a tendency to crease so it is often blended with other fibers such as cotton to make it easier to wear and work with.

## • Synthetic or Manmade Yarns

Nylon, polyester, acrylic, rayon and other synthetic fibers are easy and inexpensive to produce, and can be useful alternatives for allergy sufferers. However, they can be rather warm to wear and cheap in appearance. Nylon, acrylic and polyester are most commonly used blended with other plant or animal fibers to give stability to delicate or fragile mixes.

## • Yarn Weights

Each strand of fiber in yarn is called a ply. Different yarns are made of different numbers of plies. The type of fiber, number of plies and method of spinning all affect the thickness and weight of the finished yarn. Traditionally there were set thicknesses, such as 4-ply and chunky, but new technology has enabled a broader range of unusual yarns, and these terms have become less standardized.

The weights of yarn used in this book are:

LIGHTWEIGHT: very fine yarn designed for crochet work and used embellishment.

4-PLY: Fine yarn generally knitted on size 2 or 3 needles.

DK (DOUBLE KNITTING): Around twice the thickness of 4-ply and usually knitted on size 6 or 7 needles.

ARAN: Around twice the thickness of DK, this knits up quickly on size 8 or 9 needles.

CHUNKY: This can be anything thicker than Aran and may be knitted on needles above size 11.

## • Yarn labels

Whether it comes in ball or hank form, the yarn you buy will have a label around it that lists a lot of useful information:

**1** Company brand and yarn name.

**2** Weight and length measurements.

**3** Fiber content.

**4** Shade number and dye lot. The manufacturer's shade number refers to a specific color; the dye lot indicates a particular batch dyed in that color. When buying yarns for a project, ensure that balls of one color are all from the same dye lot. Try to keep your labels, or make a note of dye lots for reference.

**5** Needle size – a generally recommended size. Your project pattern instructions will tell you which specific size to use. Since the needles required for each project are chosen to create a particular feel to the finished fabric, they may be very different from those stated on the label.

**6** Recommended tension. This tells you the standard tension for the yarn using the recommended needle size, usually given as a number of stitches and rows measured over 4 inches (10 cm) of stockinette stitch.

**7** Washing instructions.

# Equipment

At the most basic level, all you need to create a knitted fabric are needles and yarn. As you improve your skills, however, you will soon discover that there is a whole array of materials and equipment at your disposal – from useful gadgets to make your life easier, to items that are used for very specific knitting styles or techniques. This section provides an overview of what is available.

## • Needles

Needles are available in a variety of materials; the cheapest are aluminium and plastic. They can also be made from bamboo, steel, ebony or even bone. Different materials will give you a different knitting experience, and personal preference will dictate which you choose to knit with.

The important thing is that needles are not bent, and that they do not snag the yarn while knitting. The thickness or size of a needle should be appropriate for the yarn you are using.

There are three types of needles: straight, double-pointed and circular.

### Straight needles

These come in pairs and vary from 10 to 18 inches (25 to 45 cm) in length. Make sure that the needle you are using is long enough for the width of your project. They have an end piece to stop the stitches from falling off.

circular needle

## Cable needles

These short, double-pointed needles are used to hold stitches at the back or front of the work when knitting cables. Cranked cable needles have a V-shaped bend, which stops stitches from slipping off when working the cable.

## Circular needles

These are two short needle ends joined by flexible cord, and are handy for resting bulky, or heavy projects in your lap, or when the longest straight needle is not long enough for the item being knitted.

## Double-pointed needles

Supplied in sets of four or five, these are used for knitting neckbands, and for small, seamless tubes to construct such items as socks, mittens and gloves.

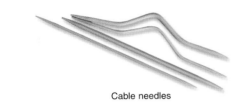
Cable needles

Straight needles and double-pointed needles

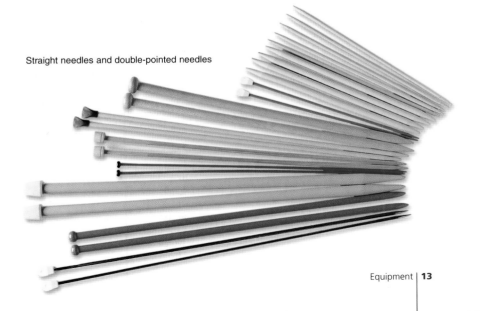

Aluminum needles

## Knitting needle sizes

| US SIZE | METRIC SIZE (mm) |
|---------|------------------|
| 0 | 2 |
| 1 | 2.25, 2.5 |
| 2 | 2.75, 3 |
| 3 | 3.25 |
| 4 | 3.5 |
| 5 | 3.75 |
| 6 | 4 |
| 7 | 4.5 |
| 8 | 5 |
| 9 | 5.5 |
| 10 | 6 |
| 10.5 | 6.5, 7, 7.5 |
| 11 | 8 |
| 13 | 9 |
| 15 | 10 |

Plastic needles

knitting very chunky yarn, and needles as small as 0 to 0000 for very fine lace knitting.

Metric needle sizes are the ones most commonly used in Europe. They give the diameter of the needle in millimeters, with sizes starting at 2 mm and going up to 20 mm.

### Needle sizes

Needles come in different diameters as well as lengths so that the knitted stitch achieves the correct gauge for the article being made. Unfortunately there is no universal size guide for knitting needles. Instead, there are two main categories: American and metric.

American needle sizes generally range from 0 to 15, with the diameter increasing as the number gets larger. It is also possible to find jumbo sized 17 and 19 needles for

Jumbo plastic needles

Bamboo needles

## • Other Essential Equipment

In addition to knitting needles, there are a few other essentials that you should have in your workbox.

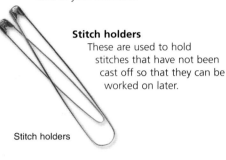

### Stitch holders
These are used to hold stitches that have not been cast off so that they can be worked on later.

Stitch holders

### Tape measure
This is an essential piece of equipment for checking gauge, and for making sure your work is the correct size.

Tape measure

Row counter

### Row counter
Place this on the end of a needle, and turn it after each row to keep count of the number of rows worked.

### Stitch markers
To mark a particular stitch or row, these colored plastic or metal rings can either be placed onto a needle or into a stitch. Alternatively, you might prefer to use scraps of contrasting colored yarn tied into a slipknot.

Stitch markers

### Crochet hook
This is handy for picking up dropped stitches, and for adding fringing to the edges of a piece of knitting.

Crochet hook

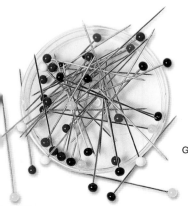

### Glass-headed pins
These dressmaking pins are used to hold pieces of knitted fabric at the correct size before pressing or steaming.

Glass-headed pins

### Scissors

These are essential for cutting. You never breatk yarn with your fingers.

Scissors

### Mohair brush

This is used to brush up mohair after knitting to increase the hairiness of the fabric.

Mohair brush

### Needles

Yarn needles have blunt tips ideal for sewing in ends and sewing seams. The eye should be large enough to thread the yarn through easily. Pointed sewing needles are useful for threading beads onto yarn, or for sewing beads onto projects after knitting.

Sewing needles

### Pompom maker

This comes in various sizes and makes it easier and quicker to create pompoms for decorative touches.

Pompom maker

### Needle gauge

A needle gauge is a handy and inexpensive tool to double-check the sizes of unmarked, or old needles.

Needle gauge

### Knitting spool

Also known as a French knitting doll, this is used to make a cord of knitted fabric. First the yarn is wrapped around a series of pegs. The bottom loops are then slipped over the top ones with a small blunt pin.

Knitting spool

### Bobbins

These hold small quantities of yarn, and are particularly useful when knitting intarsia.

### Notebook or scrapbook

This is useful for keeping a record of yarns used and dye lots, jotting down design ideas, and storing magazine clippings. It is also a good idea to make a note of any changes you make to an existing pattern for future reference.

### Point protectors

When needles are not in use, these are placed on the ends to stop stitches from dropping off. They also protect the tips of bamboo needles, which can chip or split.

Point protectors

# Getting Started

# First Steps

The first thing to ensure, before learning to knit, is that you have a comfortable, quiet space that is well lit. Make sure that the chair you are sitting in supports your back, and allows your arms to move freely. Relax – knitting should be an enjoyable experience.

Allow yourself plenty of time to get a handle on the basics. Everyone learns at a different speed, so the right pace is your pace. When learning or practicing basic techniques, choose a medium-weight yarn. This will help you feel that you are making some progress without having to work with too large a needle size.

## • Holding the Yarn

For a successful knitting project, the yarn needs to be held well. There are numerous ways of holding it; the best is the one that feels most comfortable. In the examples shown on these pages, the yarn is pulled quite tight as it passes through the hands, while leaving the fingertips free to control the needles.

### Left hand
Holding the yarn in this hand is faster because the yarn does not have as far to travel to work each stitch. Wrap the yarn around your little finger, then snake it around your other fingers in a way that feels comfortable.

### Right hand
Wrap the yarn around your little finger, then snake it over your ring ringer, under your middle finger and over your index finger.

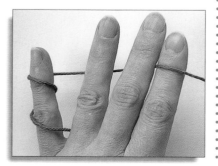

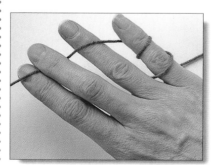

## • Holding the Needles

There are two ways in which needles can
be held: from above, known as the knife
hold, or from beneath, known as the pen
hold. The left needle is always held from
above, while the right needle can be held
either way.

### German method

This is the fastest method of knitting.
Both the needles are held from above in
the knife hold. The left hand controls the
yarn and moves the stitches on the left
needle, while the right hand moves the
right needle into and out of the stitches
on the left needle This is also known as
the continental, or left-handed method.

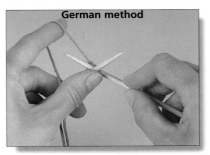

German method

### Scottish method

With this method, both needles are held
from above in the knife hold. The left
hand controls the needles, moving the
stitches toward the tip of the left needle
to be worked, and guiding the right
needle into and out of the stitches. The
right hand controls the feed of the yarn.
This is also known as the English or
fixed-needle method.

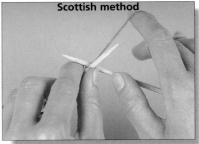

Scottish method

### French method

Although considered to be more elegant
than the German method, and similar to
the Scottish, this style is more time-
consuming. The right needle is held from
beneath in the pen hold between thumb
and index finger. The right index finger is
used to guide the yarn over the needles.
This is also known as the free-needle method.

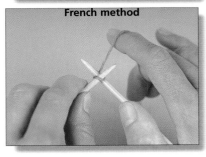

French method

# Casting On

All knitting starts with a foundation stitch called a slipknot. There are various ways of casting on, some of which are best suited to certain stitches, but generally it is a matter of personal preference.

## • Making a slipknot

The following steps show you how to make a slipknot. Once you have your slipknot, place it on the left needle to form the first cast-on stitch.

### Step 1
Make a loop by wrapping the yarn in a clockwise direction around the first three fingers of your left hand.

### Step 2
Pass the yarn held in your right hand under this loop to form another loop.

### Step 3
Remove your left hand from the first loop and pull the ends to tighten.

### Step 4
Place the loop from your right hand onto the needle and tighten. Do not pull too tight.

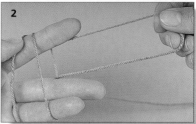

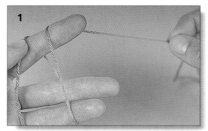

## • Cable Cast-On

This popular cast-on method uses two
needles, and creates a cabled effect along
the cast-on edge.

### Step 1
Make a slipknot and place it on the left
needle. Insert the tip of the right needle
into the slipknot from front to back.

### Step 2
Wrap the yarn counterclockwise around
the tip of the right needle. Pull the right
needle back through the slipknot,
drawing the yarn through the slipknot
to make a new stitch.

### Step 3
Transfer this stitch from the right needle
to the left, in the direction shown.

### Step 4
Use the same process to make as many
stitches as required, but from now on
insert the tip of the right needle between
the first two stitches on the left needle.
Transfer each new stitch to the left
needle as before.

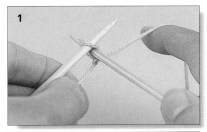

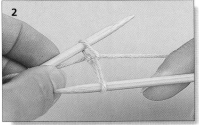

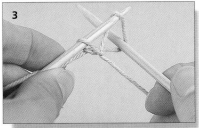

## • Casting On Using the Thumb Method

To cast on using the thumb method, you need two lengths of yarn that are worked simultaneously. The slipknot that forms the first stitch must be far enough along the yarn to create two ends – one free and the other attached to the ball.

### Step 1
Place the slipknot on the needle and hold the needle in your right hand. Take the tail end of yarn around your left thumb in a clockwise direction to form a loop.

### Step 2
Slide the needle upward through the loop on your thumb.

### Step 3
Take the yarn held in your right hand counterclockwise around the needle from back to front.

### Step 4
Bring the yarn through the loop on your thumb, release the loop and pull the end to tighten. Repeat taking the tail end of yarn around your left thumb in Step 1.

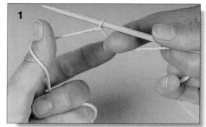

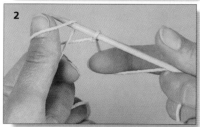

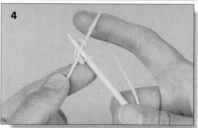

## • Long Tail Cast-On

This method is also known as the German, or double-cable, method.

### Step 1
Place the slipknot on the needle, leaving a long tail, and hold the needle in your right hand. Wrap the free end of yarn around your left thumb from front to back. Place the other yarn over your left forefinger, and hold both threads in the palm of your hand.

### Step 2
Slide the needle up through the loop on your thumb, and over the top of the yarn on your forefinger.

### Step 3
Draw the yarn through the loop on your thumb. Release the loop, and pull to tighten. Repeat from Step 1.

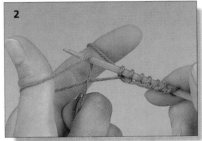

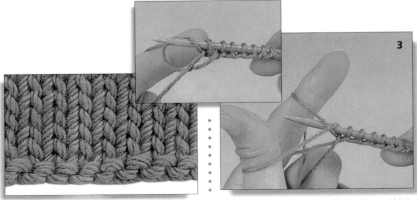

## • Invisible Cast-On

This method is worked on a single rib only. Using a contrasting thread and the cable method, cast on half the number of stitches required. An even number of stitches is needed, so cast on one extra if need be. This method is more advanced, so you may wish to return to it once you have completed a knitted piece.

### Step 1
Work a row of knit, then a row of purl in the first yarn, then work four subsequent rows of stockinette stitch in the yarn required to complete the knitted piece.

### Step 2
On the next row, purl one stitch from the left needle. Using the right needle, pick up a loop in the same color from the row where the contrast yarn finished.

### Step 3
Place the loop on the left-hand needle. Take the yarn to the back of the work and knit the stitch.

### Step 4
Purl the next stitch on the left needle, then pick up the next loop along from the row where the color changed. Repeat steps 3 and 4.

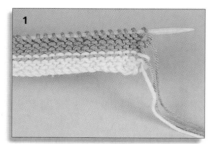

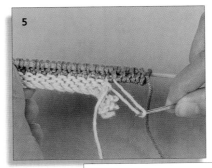

## Step 5

When the row is completed, unravel the contrast yarn.

# How to Knit a Stitch

There are two basic knitting stitches – knit and purl. However complicated the finished appearance of the knitted fabric, it will always have been produced using one or both of these stitches.

To knit a stitch, you use the right needle to pull a loop of yarn toward you through the stitch on the left needle. To practice the knit stitch, begin first by casting on about 20 stitches (see *Casting On*, pages 22–27).

## Step 1

Hold the needle with the cast-on stitches in your left hand, with the first stitch about 1 inch (2.5 cm) from the tip. Take up the ball yarn in your right hand and hold it together with the empty needle, held as you would a knife. Insert the tip of the right needle from left to right through the first stitch on the left needle, under the left needle, and in front of the yarn held in your right hand.

## Step 2

With your right forefinger carry the yarn counterclockwise over the tip of the right needle, and then between the two needles from left to right. Use the tip of the right needle to pull the loop of yarn forward through the first stitch on the left needle.

## Step 3

Slip the original stitch off the left needle. The newly made knit stitch is on the right needle. One knit stitch has been worked.

## • German (Continental) Method

If you choose to knit using the German, or continental, method (see page 21), the yarn is held in your left hand, and the stitches are worked in a different way.

**Step 1**
Hold the yarn at the back of the work, and over your index finger.

**Step 2**
Insert the right needle up through the first stitch from front to back. Take the right needle around behind the yarn on your left finger from right to left.

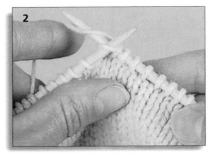

**Step 3**
Using the right needle, draw the yarn through the center of the stitch on the left needle.

**Step 4**
Slip the original stitch from the left needle, leaving the new stitch on the right needle.

# How to Purl a Stitch

The purl stitch is the second fundamental knitting stitch. To purl a stitch, you use the right needle to pull a loop of yarn away from you through the stitch on the left needle. The result is the same as a knit stitch with the wrong side facing you: a knit stitch made backward. As before, to practice the purl stitch begin first by casting on about 20 stitches (see *Casting On*, pages 22–27).

**Step 1**
Hold the needle with the stitches on in your left hand, and the empty needle in your right hand together with the yarn. Hold the yarn in front of the right needle, and insert the tip of the right needle into the first stitch on the left needle, from right to left, in front of the left needle.

**Step 2**
Use your right forefinger to wrap the yarn counterclockwise around the right needle tip as shown.

**Step 3**
With the tip of the right needle, pull the loop of yarn back through the stitch.

**Step 4**
Slip the original stitch off the left needle. The newly made purl stitch is on the right needle. One purl stitch has been worked.

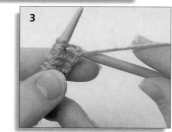

## • German (Continental) Method

If you choose to knit using the German, or continental, method, the yarn is held in your left hand, and the stitches are worked in a different way.

### Step 1
Hold the yarn at the front of the work and under your left thumb.

### Step 2
Insert the right needle up through the first stitch on the left needle from right to left, under the yarn held by your thumb, thus making a loop around the needle.

### Step 3
Using the right needle, push the looped yarn backward through the original stitch.

### Step 4
Slip the original stitch from the left needle, leaving the new stitch on the right needle.

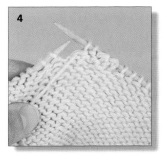

# Continuing to Knit

## • Turning the Work

At the end of every row, whether it has been a knit or a purl row, you will need to turn the work in order to start the next row. This means that the left needle becomes empty as the stitches are worked onto the right needle, and that the left needle is then transferred to the right hand to begin the next row.

In some cases, such as short row shaping, the knitter may be instructed to turn the work partway through a row. In this case simply turn the work around so that the opposite side is facing, and work the row as instructed.

## • Joining New Yarn

Whenever a ball of yarn is about to run out, join a new one at the beginning of a row. Always avoid joining a new ball of yarn halfway through a row.

To help keep good gauge when starting a new yarn, tie it around the original yarn (the knot can be undone when you are sewing in the ends of yarn after you have finished the piece). Without breaking off the yarn used for the previous row, tie the new yarn around the end of the old yarn, leaving a tail about 6 inches (15 cm) long.

Slide the knot up to the next stitch, and work the row using the new yarn. Hold the tail of the yarn out of the way for the first few stitches.

## • The Right and the Wrong Side

To create knitted projects, you need to be able to differentiate between the appearance of a knit and a purl stitch, and the right and the wrong sides of the work.

Garter stitch (shown below) is created by working knit or purl stitches only on every row. It produces quite an elastic but dense fabric. Both sides of the fabric look the same. The right and wrong side can be determined by the cast-on row, or by placing a marker of some kind.

Stockinette stitch (below) is created by working a knit row, and then a purl row in repeats. Here you can clearly see the difference between knit and purl. In stockinette stitch, one side of the work is smooth and the other slightly bumpy.

If the smooth side is facing you, the next row should be a knit row; if the bumpy side is facing you, then the next row should be purl. Stockinette stitch can also be used on the reverse, known as reverse stitch.

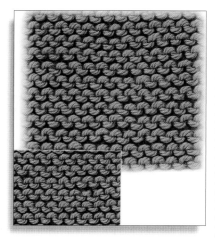

Garter stitch: Both sides are the same

Stockinette stitch:
The inset shows the wrong side

# Binding Off

Once the knitted piece has reached the required length, it needs to be bound off, or left on a holder. Without some kind of finishing, a knitted fabric will unravel. There are many different methods, but all need to be neat, slightly elastic, yet firm.

## • Basic Knit Bind-off

This is the most common binding-off technique.

**Step 1**
Knit the first two stitches from the left needle onto the right. With the yarn at the back, insert the left needle through the base of the first stitch on the right needle from left to right.

**Step 2**
Pick up the stitch, bring it over the top of the second stitch, and slip it off the right needle.

**Step 3**
With one stitch remaining on the right needle, knit the next stitch from the left needle and repeat until one stitch remains. Cut the yarn, leaving a 6-inch (15-cm) tail, draw the tail through the last stitch and pull it tight.

## • Basic Purl Bind-off

This technique creates the same firm edge as the basic knit bind-off, but is done on a purl row.

**Step 1**
Purl the first two stitches from the left needle onto the right. With the yarn at the back, insert the left needle through the base of the first stitch on the right needle from left to right.

**Step 2**
Pick up the stitch, bring it over the top of the second stitch, and slip it off the right needle.

**Step 3**
With one stitch remaining on the right needle and with the yarn at the front, purl the next stitch from the left needle and repeat.Fasten off the last stitch in the same way as step 3 in the basic knit bind-off.

## • Binding off in Rib

Rib (see pages 156–163) is mostly used to create an elastic edge around the bottom, cuff or neckline of a garment. When binding off, it is best to do so in pattern – in other words, to bind off the purl stitches purlwise and the knit stitches knitwise. This keeps the elasticity, and prevents the rib from becoming too light.

### TIP

*Once the knitted piece has been bound off, you will often find that you are left with an oversized, or "baggy," last stitch. If the piece is going to be joined to another one (for example, as a side seam), this is not a problem as the stitch will be lost in the sewing up. However, there are times when the whole bind-off is visible, such as on a blanket or small bag, and so the final stitch needs to be neat.*

*To do this, bind off every stitch except the last one. Transfer this stitch to the right needle. Using the left needle, pick up the stitch directly under the last. Transfer the slipped stitch back to the left needle, and knit off the two stitches together.*

# Understanding Gauge

Correct gauge is the key to knitting pieces to the correct size. The gauge of a knitted piece is a measure of the actual size of the knitted stitches, expressed as the number of stitches to a given width and the number of rows to a given length.

Most knitting pattern instructions include a recommended gauge, and it is vital that you match this gauge exactly, otherwise your work will be the wrong size. A recommended gauge on a yarn label or in a pattern instruction is chosen to give a correct "handle" to the work – too tight, and the work will be stiff and heavy, too loose, and it will tend to drop out of shape. So even if you compensate for incorrect gauge by working more or less rows or stitches, you may still be disappointed with the result.

## • Factors Affecting Gauge

Gauge is affected by the type of yarn used, the size of the needles, the individual knitter and the stitch pattern, and is crucial to the success of your work.

### Yarn Used

Two knitted pieces in different weights of yarn, with the same number of stitches and rows, and on the same size needles, will differ in size. Always try to obtain the exact yarn quoted in the pattern instructions. Yarns with the same general description, e.g., "worsted," may differ slightly in weight from one manufacturer, or one fiber content, to another.

## Needle Size

Two knitted pieces in exactly the same yarn, with the same number of stitches and rows, but done on different sizes of needles, will also differ in size. The larger the needles, the larger the individual stitches will be. Even the types of needles used can affect gauge. Different yarn fibers slip with varying degrees of ease over needle surfaces of plastic, wood or steel. Always use the same pair of needles for the gauge test piece as for the final knitted piece.

## The Individual Knitter

How you hold the yarn and needles in your hands also affects the gauge. Some knitters find that they consistently need larger or smaller needles than stated in the pattern to obtain a correct gauge.

## Stitch Pattern

Two knitted pieces made with exactly the same yarn, the same number of stitches and rows, and on the same-size needles will differ in size if the stitch pattern used is different. Some stitch patterns shrink, or stretch the knitting sideways, and some shrink or stretch it lengthwise. The block stitch shown below has several more rows to 4 inches (10 cm) than an equivalent piece of stockinette stitch.

## • Measuring Gauge

Before beginning any new project, knit a test piece in the following way.

### Step 1

Read the pattern instructions to find the recommended gauge. This will usually be quoted as "x stitches and y rows to 4 inches (10 cm)," measured over a certain stitch pattern and using a certain size of needles.

### Step 2

Using the yarn that you intend to use for your knitted piece, and the needle size specified, cast on a few more stitches than the figure quoted, enough to make the test piece about 6 inches (15 cm) wide. If you are working a particular stitch pattern, choose a number to suit the stitch repeat. Work in the required stitch pattern for about 6 inches (15 cm), and bind off. Block this test piece (see *Assembly section*) in the way you intend to block the finished piece.

### Step 3

Lay the test piece right side up on a flat surface, and use a ruler or tape measure to insert two pins exactly 4 inches (10 cm) apart at the center of the piece, along a straight row of stitches. Make a note of the number of stitches between the pins, including any half-stitches. This is the number of stitches to 4 inches (10 cm).

### Step 4

In the same way, measure off 4 inches (10 cm) vertically, inserting two pins exactly 4 inches (10 cm) apart at the center of the piece, along a straight line of stitches. Make a note of the number of rows between the pins, including any half-rows. This is the number of rows to 4 inches (10cm). Depending on the yarn and stitch pattern, it may be easier to turn the test piece over and measure the rows on the reverse side. If your gauge matches the recommended gauge exactly, congratulations! If not, you must adjust your gauge as described.

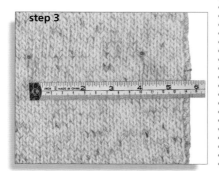

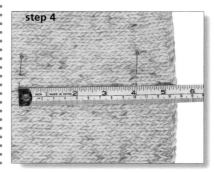

## • Adjusting Gauge

If your test piece has too many stitches or rows to 4 inches (10 cm), your work is too tight and you must work another test piece using larger needles. If your test piece has too few stitches or rows, the work is too loose. Work another test piece, using smaller needles.

Block or press the new test-piece as before and measure the gauge as opposite. Repeat this process until your gauge is exactly right. Remember that a difference of one stitch or row over 4 inches (10 cm) can translate into a difference of 3 to 4 inches (7.5 to 10 cm) over the width or length of a complete garment, so it is important to get the gauge right.

## • Substituting Yarns

Sometimes it is not possible to find the exact yarn specified in the pattern instructions, because manufacturers discontinue lines and colors for various reasons. Read the pattern instructions carefully and note the recommended gauge and needle size, the yarn's fiber content, and the yardage, if quoted. If necessary, try to find another yarn to match all these criteria as closely as possible, the most important factor being the gauge.

If possible, buy just one ball and make one or more test pieces, matching the gauge before purchasing the bulk of the yarn. If the substitute yarn quotes a shorter yardage on the yarn label than the recommended yarn, extra yarn will be required. As a rule, cotton and cotton-blend yarns are particularly heavy and therefore have a shorter yardage.

# Increasing

There are many different way to shape your knitting, including increasing the number of stitches – gradually (single stitch increasing) or more drastically (multiple stitch increasing).

## • Increase One Knitwise

This increase can be worked anywhere on a row, and involves knitting into a stitch twice in order to make an extra stitch.

**Step 1**
Work to the point in the row where you need to increase. Knit into the front of the stitch on the left needle in the usual way, but do not slip it off the left needle when you have finished.

**Step 2**
Keeping the original stitch on the left needle, and the yarm at the back of the work, knit into the back of the stitch – you have now increased one stitch. Slip the stitch from the left needle.

## • Increase One Purlwise

This increase can be worked anywhere on a row, and involves purling into a stitch twice in order to make an extra stitch.

### Step 1
Work to the point in the row where you need to increase. Purl into the front of the stitch on the left needle in the usual way, but do not slip it off the left needle when you have finished.

### Step 2
Keeping the original stitch on the left needle and the yarn at the front of the work, purl into the back of the stitch – you have now increased one stitch. Slip the stitch from the left needle.

## • Make One Knitwise

This increase uses the horizontal bar that lies between pairs of stitches to create a new stitch. It can be worked anywhere on a row.

### Step 1
Work to the point in the row where you need to increase. Insert the tip of the right needle underneath the horizontal bar lying between the last stitch on the right needle, and the first stitch slip on the left needle.

### Step 2
Lift this bar and slip it onto the left needle. Knit into the back of this loop to create a new stitch, slipping the lifted loop off the left needle when you have finished.

## • Make Two Knitwise

This increase is best worked at either the beginning or the end of the knitted piece, as it is not particularly neat. Use it on the edge, or one stitch in from the edge, so that it will be lost when the pieces are sewn together.

### Step 1
Work to where the extra stitch is needed. Knit into the front and back of the next stitch on the left knitting needle without slipping it off.

### Step 2
With the stitch still on the left needle and the yarn at the back, knit into the front of the stitch again, and slip it from the needle.

An increase made by making two knitwise; that is, knitting into the front and the back of a stitch.

## • Make One Purlwise

This increase is worked anywhere on a row, and again uses the horizontal bar that lies between pairs of stitches to create a new stitch. Repeat steps 1 and 2 of "Make One Knitwise" (on page 43), but purl into the back of the lifted loop instead of knitting into it.

## • Make Two Purlwise

Follow the instructions for "Make One Purlwise," but do not slip the lifted loop off the left needle after you have purled into the back of it. Now insert the right needle into the front of the loop and purl the stitch. You have now made two new stitches. Slip the loop off the left needle.

### TIP: HOLDING STITCHES

*Some projects require stitches to be left on a holder to be worked at a later stage in the pattern. Simply insert the pin of the holder from right to left through each stitch, taking care not to twist them. When you need to work on these stitches, slip them from the holder onto a knitting needle, again taking care not to twist them.*

# Decreasing

As with increasing, there are numerous methods of decreasing in order to shape a piece of knitting, either gradually by knitting stitches together, or more sharply by binding stitches off.

## • Knit Two Together (abbreviated K2tog)

This creates a slope to the right on the face of the fabric.

**Step 1**
Work to where you need to decrease. Insert the tip of the right needle knitwise into the front of the first two stitches on the left needle.

**Step 2**
Knit the two stitches together as if they were a single stitch. You have now decreased one stitch.

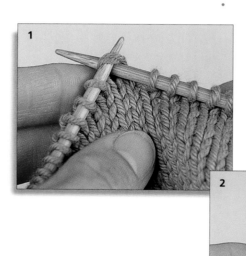

## • Knit Two Together through Back Loops (abbreviated K2tog tbl)

This creates a slope to the left on the face of the fabric.

### Step 1
Work to where you need to decrease. Insert the tip of the right needle knitwise into the back of the first two stitches on the left needle.

### Step 2
Knit the two stitches together as if they were a single stitch. You have now decreased one stitch.

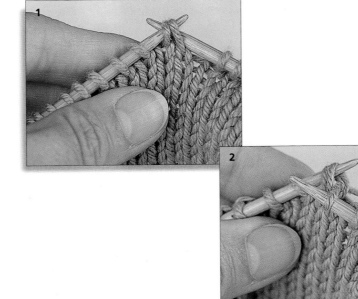

## • Purl Two Together (abbreviated P2tog)

Worked on a wrong side row, this creates a slope to the right on the face of the fabric.

**Step 1**
Work to where you need to decrease. Insert the tip of the right needle purlwise into the front of the first two stitches on the left needle.

**Step 2**
Purl the two stitches together as if they were a single stitch. You have now decreased one stitch.

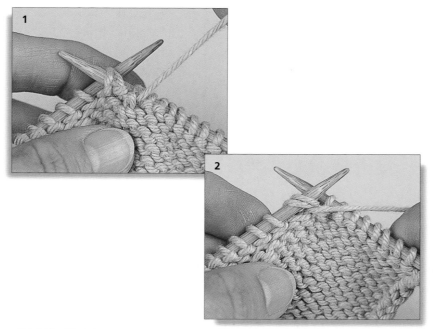

## • Purl Two Together through Back Loops (abbreviated P2tog tbl)

Worked on a wrong side row, this creates a slope to the left on the face of the fabric.

**Step 1**
Work to where you need to decrease. Insert the tip of the right needle purlwise into the back of the first two stitches on the left needle.

**Step 2**
Purl the two stitches together as if they were a single stitch. You have now decreased one stitch.

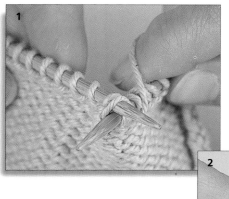

## • Slip Stitch Decreasing

Skpo (slip one, knit one, pass slipped stitch over) is a method of decreasing that is often used when making lace holes. It creates a slope to the left on the face of the fabric.

### Step 1
Insert the tip of the right needle knitwise into the first stitch on the left needle and slip the stitch from the left to the right needle without working it.

### TIP:
### FULLY FASHIONED SHAPING

*Visible shaping, where the increases and the decreases are worked a few stitches in from the edges of the knitting, is known as fully fashioned shaping. Working into the front or back of stitches that are knitted or purled together emphasizes the way the knitting is shaped or "fashioned," and many of the projects in this book use this as a decorative feature.*

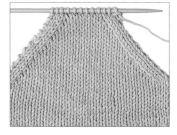

### Step 2
Knit the next stitch on the left needle in the usual way, then insert the tip of the left needle into the slipped stitch on the right needle. Lift the slipped stitch over the knitted stitch, and drop it off the right needle.

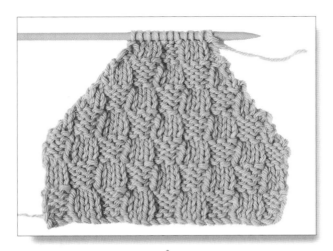

## TIP:
## KEEPING PATTERNS CONSTANT

When decreasing (or increasing for that matter) at the same time as working in a stitch pattern, it is important to keep the stitch pattern correct. A stitch pattern as written row by row at the beginning of knitting instructions will not always fit into the differing numbers of stitches on each row as shaping proceeds. The instructions for the block pattern piece shown might read: Keeping pattern constant, decrease 1 stitch at each end next and every alternate row.

Learn to look at the stitch you are working on, and understand how it is constructed. In this block pattern example, each block consists of three stitches and four rows. These blocks of stockinette stitch, and reverse stockinette stitch are arranged in a checkerboard fashion.

So as the shaping proceeds, blocks at the edges are reduced from three stitches to two, then to one stitch, then the next block of three stitches becomes the edge block, but the pattern remains constant.

With complicated stitch patterns, the instructions usually include row-by-row directions for the shaping rows. Follow these instructions carefully and examine the result to make sure your interpretation is correct. You should not wait until the very end before thinking about the pattern's development.

# Other Stitch Techniques

Having covered the basics of knitting, purling, increasing and decreasing, you will find that patterns use many variations on these instructions to create special effects. This section outlines some of the most popular stitches and their techniques.

## • Slipping a Stitch

To slip a stitch, just move it from the left to the right needle without working it. When this is done as part of a stitch pattern, the stitch is usually slipped purlwise, so that the stitch lies on the needle in the same direction as an ordinary knit stitch.

Slipping stitches makes a close, firm fabric. If the stitch is slipped purlwise on a right-side row with the yarn at the back, the design is vertical. If the stitch is slipped purlwise on a right-side row with the yarn at the front, the design is horizontal.

Stitches can also be slipped purlwise on wrong-side rows. If the wrong-side row is purled, and the yarn is held in front, the strand won't show on the right side; if the yarn is held at the back, the strand will show on the right side.

### Step 1
To slip one purlwise with yarn at the back on a knit row, insert the right needle into the stitch as if to purl, then slip the stitch from the left to the right needle, as shown below. Do not take the yarn around the needle – there is no new stitch.

### Step 2
To slip one knitwise with yarn in front on a knit row, bring the yarn to the front of the work, insert the right needle into the stitch as if to purl, then slip the stitch from the left to right needle, as shown below. Take the yarn to the back of the work.

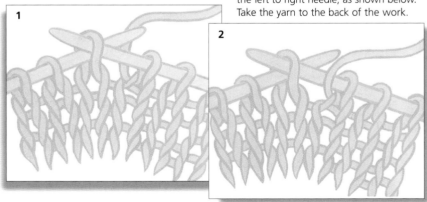

## • Working into the Back of a Stitch

This is often used to add definition to a stitch pattern. It closes up the V shape on the right side of the fabric, and makes the diagonals from bottom right to top left more prominent. As the knitting progresses, these diagonals emphasize the verticals on the right side of the fabric.

### Step 1
To knit into the back of a stitch (k1tbl), insert the right needle into the back of the stitch from right to left, take the yarn around the needle and make the new stitch in the usual way.

### Step 2
To purl into the back of a stitch (p1tbl), swing the needle ends slightly away from you to insert the right needle into the back of the stitch from left to right. Then take the yarn around the needle, and make a new stitch in the usual way.

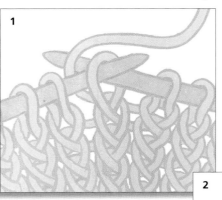

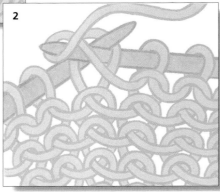

## • Drop Stitches

These are formed by wrapping the yarn
twice around the right needle instead of
once, and dropping the extra loop on the
following row. This technique is always
done knitwise in this book, and is used
for one, two or more stitches at a time.

### Step 1
Knit the next stitch, wrapping the yarn
around the needle twice.

### Step 2
Pull the double loop through as you
complete the knit stitch.

### Step 3
On the following row, work the double
loop as instructed in the pattern, allowing
the extra loop to drop from the left
needle as you do so.

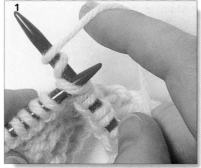

## • Make one stitch by Yarn-Over (yo)

A yarn-over increase is made by simply winding the yarn once around the right needle. This creates a hole or eyelet in the knitting. Be careful to wind yarn-overs correctly, as shown below – if they twist the wrong way, the following row will be difficult to work, and the appearance of the stitch pattern will be affected.

### A yarn-over between two knit stitches

**Step 1**
Bring the yarn forward between the needles, then return it to the back of the work over the top of the right needle. The yarn is now wrapped from front to back around the right needle, and in the correct position to knit the next stitch.

**Step 2**
Knit the next stitch in the usual way and complete the row. This yarn over creates a hole between two knit stitches.

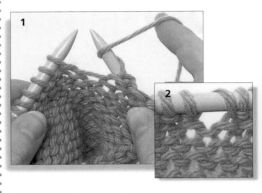

### A yarn-over between two purl stitches

**Step 1**
Take the yarn to the back of the work over the top of the right needle.

**Step 2**
Bring it forward between the needles. The yarn is now wrapped from front to back around the right needle, and in the correct position to purl the next stitch. This yarn over creates a hole between two purl stitches.

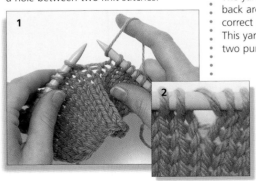

## Yarn-over after a knit stitch and before a purl stitch

### Step 1
Bring the yarn forward between the needles.

### Step 2
Take the yarn to the back over the top of the right needle, and forward again between the needles. The yarn is now in the correct position for purling the next stitch. This yarn-over creates a hole between a knit stitch and a purl stitch.

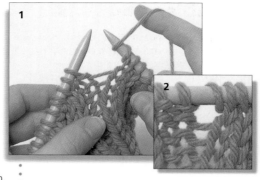

## Yarn-over after a purl stitch and before a knit stitch

### Step 1
The yarn is in the forward position after working a purl stitch. Take it to the back over the top of the right needle. Beware! If you take the yarn back between the needles you will not create an extra stitch.

### Step 2
Knit the next stitch. This yarn over creates a hole between a purl stitch and a knit stitch (shown inset).

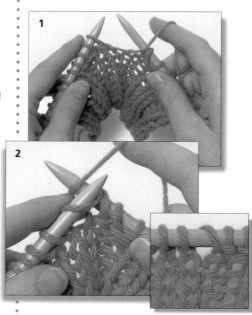

# Cables and Twists

Different arrangements of cables and twists, crossed from right to left or from left to right, give rise to many interesting stitch patterns, such as those used on traditional Aran knitting.

Cables are formed by crossing one group of stitches over another at regular intervals such as every four, six or eight rows. Each group may be two, three or more stitches. A cable of two groups of two stitches is called a four-stitch cable. The examples below are six-stitch cables, worked with two groups of three stitches. Cables are worked with the help of a cable needle: a short double-pointed needle, about 4 inches (10 cm) long. It may be straight or shaped with a kink in the middle ("cranked") to prevent stitches from slipping off. Choose a cable needle slightly smaller in size than the main needles in use to avoid stretching the stitches.

## • Cable to right (six-stitch cable shown, abbreviated C6R)

### Step 1
On a right-side row, work to the position required for the cable. Holding the cable needle at the front of the work, insert it purlwise into the first group (three stitches), slipping them one by one off the left needle.

### Step 2
Keeping the cable needle at the back of the work, knit the next group (next 3 stitches). Then knit the group of stitches on the cable needle, beginning with the first stitch slipped. The cable twists to the right. The cable shown here was worked on every eighth row.

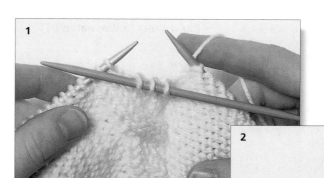

## • Cable to left (six-stitch cable shown, abbreviated C6L)

### Step 1
On a right-side row, work to the position required for the cable. Holding the cable needle at the front of the work, insert it purlwise into the first group (three stitches), slipping them one by one off the left needle.

### Step 2
Keeping the cable needle at the front of the work, knit the next group (next three stitches).

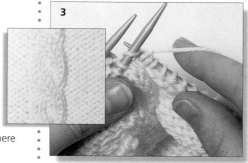

### Step 3
Then knit the group of stitches on the cable needle, beginning with the first stitch slipped. The cable twists to the left. The cable shown here was worked on every eighth row.

Twists are simply made up of two stitches worked in such a way as to twist either to the right or the left. No cable needle is necessary.

## • Left twist (abbreviated LT)

### Step 1
On a right-side row, work to the required position. Skip the first stitch on the left needle, and insert the right needle into the back of the second stitch, behind the first stitch. Wrap the yarn knitwise and pull through a loop, leaving the second stitch on the left needle.

### Step 2
Insert the right needle through the back loops of the first and second stitches together, wrap the yarn knitwise, and pull through another loop, slipping both stitches off the left needle.

Moving the position of the left twist by one stitch to the left on every right-side row creates a diagonal line sloping up to the left.

## • Right twist (abbreviated RT)

### Step 1
On a right-side row, work to the required position. Insert the right needle knitwise into the first two stitches together. Wrap the yarn knitwise and pull through a loop, leaving both stitches on the left needle.

### Step 2
Knit the first stitch again in the usual way.

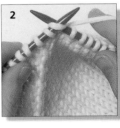

### Step 3
Slip both stitches off the left needle. Moving the position of the right twist by one stitch to the right on every right-side row creates a diagonal line sloping up to the right.

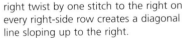

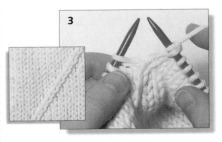

# Bobbles

This round ball is created by working on a small number of stitches within the knitted piece to make a section that stands in relief. Bobbles can also be knitted separately and sewn on once the main piece is completed (see page 79).

## • To make a bobble within a knitted piece

### Step 1
Work to where the bobble is to be placed. Increase the next stitch by knitting into the front and then the back of the stitch until you have the required number of stitches (the more stitches and rows you work, the bigger the bobble). About four or five stitches will probably be sufficient.

### Step 2
Work on these stitches only in either stockinette or garter stitch, for five or seven rows, ending with a wrong-side row. Turn the work.

### Step 3
Slip all the stitches used to make the bobble over the top of the first. Work to the end of the row as required.

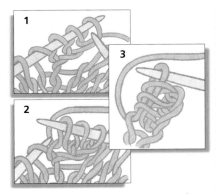

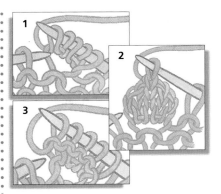

Here are two more typical methods of working bobbles.

## • Making a Three-stitch Bobble

This bobble is small and created over three stitches.

**Step 1**
Work to where you want the bobble. Work into the next stitch on the left needle, and create extra stitches by casting on three stitches.

**Step 2**
Knit the three cast-on stitches, then knit the original stitch again, making four new stitches on the right needle.

**Step 3**
To complete the bobble, lift the three stitches, one at a time, over the last stitch on the right needle.

## • Making a Five-stitch Bobble

This example is on a reverse stockinette stitch background.

**Step 1**
Work to where you want the bobble. Work into the next stitch on the left needle and create extra stitches by working into the front and back of this stitch until five stitches are on the right needle.

**Step 2**
Turn and purl the five stitches.

**Step 3**
To complete the bobble, turn, knit five stitches, turn, purl two stitches together, purl one stitch, then purl two stitches together, turn, slip two stitches knitwise, knit one, then pass the slipped stitches over the last knit stitch. Alternatively, you can decrease the five stitches by working all five stitches together at once so that only one stitch remains.

# Assembly

Now that you have completed your project, you have come to the task that a lot of knitters hate – sewing in ends, pressing and sewing seams. Having knitted your items with such care, take your time.

## • Sewing in Ends

Yarn ends are left whenever you change color, join a new ball or sew seams. Always leave a tail end of yarn about 6 inches (15 cm) long so that you can sew it neatly into the knitting. Undo any knots joining yarns, then thread the yarn end through a yarn needle.

### Along a seam
Run the needle in and out of the stitches inside the seam at the edge of the knitting for about 3 inches (7.5 cm). Pull the yarn through and trim the end.

### Along a row

**Step 1**
Run the needle in and out of the back of stitches of the same color, working along the row for about four to six stitches.

**Step 2**
Take the needle back, catching in the sewn-in yarn for two to three stitches. Stretch the knitting widthwise, and trim the end of the yarn.

**1**

**2**

## • Blocking and Pressing

Blocking is the term used for pinning out each knitted piece to the correct size before pressing. You can use an ironing board for small pieces, or make a blocking board by placing a thin layer of wadding on top of a sheet of hardboard. Cover this with a piece of checkered fabric stretched tautly and pinned, or taped securely to the hardboard. The checks will help you to lay the work straight.

### Step 1
Check your pattern for the finished measurements. Using large glass-headed pins and with the wrong side of the knitting facing upward, pin the pieces out to the correct dimensions, taking care not to stretch the knitting out of shape.

### Step 2
Place a damp cloth over the fabric and press with an iron set at the correct temperature for the yarn used. Do not apply too much pressure, or you will flatten the texture of the knitting. For cabled or highly textured pieces, hold a steam iron about 1 to 2 inches (2.5 to 5 cm) above the surface, and allow the steam to penetrate the fabric. Avoid pressing or steaming rib because this causes it to lose elasticity.

## • Sewing Up

Sewing up from the right side is the secret of invisible seams. This method, also known as "ladder stitch" or "mattress stitch," is good for joining side and sleeve seams in most stitch patterns.

### Invisible seam

Place both pieces of knitting flat, with right sides facing, and the edges to be joined running vertically. Thread a yarn needle with yarn and secure at one lower edge – the first side. Take the needle under the cast-on edge of the second side, draw the yarn through, then go under the first cast-on edge again. Gauge the yarn to level the edges. Take the needle under the strand between the edge stitch, and the next stitch on the first row of the second side, and draw the yarn through. Repeat for the first row of the first side. Continue joining row ends from alternate sides in this way, without splitting stitches.

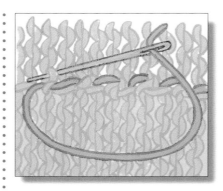

### Slip stitch

Catching down pocket linings, or zipper facings is easy with slip stitches. With wrong sides facing, baste the pieces to be joined, matching rows. Thread a yarn needle with yarn. Secure the end, then take the needle alternately under a strand on the main fabric and an edge strand. Don't let the stitches show on the right side or pull the yarn too tight.

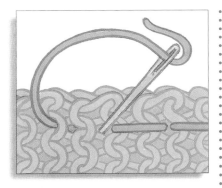

### Back stitch

Back stitching makes strong seams. Hold the pieces with right sides together. Thread a yarn needle and secure the yarn at the right-hand end. Lining up rows and working one stitch in from the edge, bring the needle up through both pieces of knitting between stitches of the first and second rows, then down between the first row and the cast-on edge. Come up again one or two rows further, and go down next to the previous stitch. Complete the seam in this way, taking care to work between the knitted stitches.

## • Picking up Stitches

Most knitted pieces have an edging or border of some kind to neaten the edge and prevent the fabric from curling. While lace edgings and tassel-type edgings are generally sewn onto the piece, ribs and bands tend to be worked by picking up stitches.

Stitches must be picked up evenly, particularly around necklines since this tends to be the focal point of a garment. Your pattern tells you how many stitches are needed for an even pickup, but remember that if the length or size of the garment has been changed, the number of stitches for the pickup will alter, too. If too few stitches are used, the knitted piece will pucker, and if too many are picked up then the band will flare.

Stitches are picked up either through the whole or half of the edge stitch, using a knitting needle or crochet hook two sizes smaller than that used to knit the bulk of the piece.

### Marking the edge for picking up stitches

Measure the edge of the knitted piece and place large-ended pins, markers or short knotted pieces of yarn at even intervals – for example, every 2 inches (5 cm). To calculate how many stitches to pick up between the markers, divide the number of sections into the number of stitches required.

## Picking up stitches along a horizontal edge

To pick up along a bound-off edge such as around a blanket, one needle is used and the right side of the work faces you.

### Step 1
Hold the needle in your right hand and insert it through the center of the first stitch below the bind-off from front to back.

### Step 2
Wrap the new yarn around the knitting needle from back to front, as if to knit.

### Step 3
Pull the loop through the knitted stitch to the front.

## Picking up stitches along a vertical edge

This is done one stitch in from the edge of the knitted piece, with one needle and the right side of the work facing you.

### Step 1
Insert the knitting needle between the first and second stitches at the bottom corner of the knitted piece.

### Step 2
Wrap the yarn around the knitting needle from back to front, and pull the loop through the knitted piece. Repeat as required.

## Picking up stitches along a shaped edge

When picking up stitches around a neckline or any piece of shaped knitting, pick up one stitch in from the edge to eliminate jagged or untidy shaping.

Be very careful when picking up between the knitted piece, and any stitches that have been left on stitch holders or have not been bound off (at the center of the neck, for example). Do not pick up into the center of any obvious holes.

If the neckband is a different color than the body of the piece, pick up the stitches in the main color, and change yarns for the first row.

## Picking up stitches with a crochet hook

### Step 1
Insert the crochet hook through the knitted piece from front to back between the first two stitches, or into the center of the stitch below the bind-off.

### Step 2
Wrap the yarn around the hook from front to back and pull through. Repeat until all stitches have been made.

### Step 3
Once complete, slip the loops onto a knitting needle, making sure that they are not twisted.

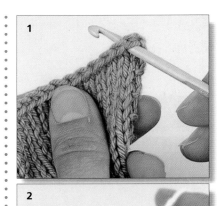

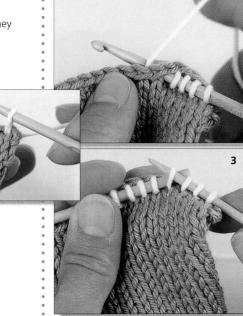

# Correcting Mistakes

## • Picking up Dropped Garter Stitches

If you drop a stitch while you are knitting, you can pick it up, and no one will ever know. Try to pick up a dropped stitch as soon as possible, or it will keep running further down and potentially be more difficult to fix.

**Step 1**
Put the tip of the right needle through the dropped stitch, from back to front.

**Step 2**
Insert the tip of the right needle under the strand, from back to front.

**Step 3**
Use the point of your left needle to lift the dropped stitch over the strand, and drop it off the right needle, like binding off. The new stitch is now on the right needle.

**Step 4**
Insert the point of the left needle into the new stitch from front to back and slip the stitch onto the left needle, ready to be knitted as usual.

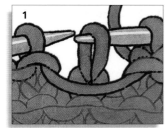

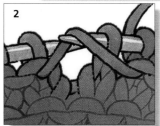

## • Picking up Dropped Stockinette Stitches

### On a Knit Row

**Step 1**
Hold the knitting with the knit side facing you.

**Step 2**
Insert the tip of the right-hand needle through the dropped stitch from front to back, and then under the strand above it in the same way, from front to back.

**Step 3**
Use the point of the left needle to lift the picked-up stitch, pass it over the strand and off the needle, just like binding off, leaving the repaired stitch on the right needle.

**Step 4**
Put the tip of the left needle through the repaired stitch from front to back, and slip the stitch onto the left needle, ready to be worked in the usual way.

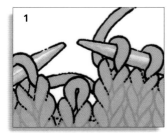

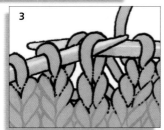

## On a Purl Row

### Step 1
Hold the piece of knitting with the purl side facing you.

### Step 2
Insert the tip of the right needle through the dropped stitch from back to front, and then insert the tip of the needle under the strand above it the same way.

### Step 3
Use the point of the left needle to lift the picked-up stitch and pass it over the strand and off the needle, just like binding off, leaving the repaired stitch on the right needle.

### Step 4
Put the tip of the left needle through the repaired stitch from front to back and slip the stitch onto the left needle, ready to be worked in the usual way.

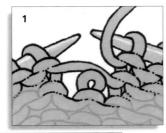

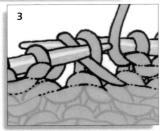

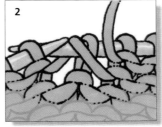

# Finishing
# Techniques

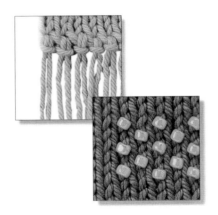

# Selvages

The selvage is the very edge stitch or stitches of the knitted fabric. Most written patterns assume that the edge stitch will be worked in a pattern – that is, knitted on a knit row and purled on a purl row. However, this is a matter of personal choice.

There are ways to work these edge stitches to create neater or decorative edges that prevent the work from curling, and make it easier to sew together. Patterns usually allow for a selvage stitch to ensure that ribs and color match up correctly when sewn together.

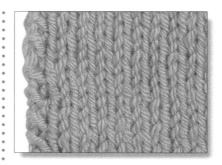

## • Garter Stitch Selvage

This is the most common selvage used on stockinette stitch fabrics, as well as other stitch patterns where pieces are to be joined using an invisible seam (see page 64).The garter stitch selvage makes the edge stitches slightly firmer, avoiding an uneven appearance. To work this selvage, simply work the first and last stitch of every row as a knit stitch.

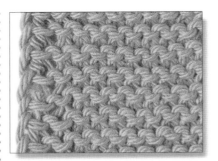

## • Slip Stitch Selvage

This selvage is popular with some knitters because it creates a neat edge that is ideal for pieces that do not need to be sewn together, such as scarves and blankets. However, because a row of knitting is missed on one stitch, it can make holes and create problems when picking up stitches. To work a slip stitch selvage, simply slip the first stitch on every row to pattern – that is, knitwise on a knit row and purlwise on a purl row.

## • Chain Stitch Selvage

This selvage is used to form a neat edge on garter stitch (all rows knit), where both edges will be left free, as for a strap, or only one edge will be left free, as at the front edge of a cardigan.

### Chain stitch selvage on both edges

Row 1: Bring the yarn forward in front of the right needle. Insert the right needle into the first stitch from right to left (purlwise) and slip the first stitch onto the right needle. Take the yarn to the back between the needles, and knit to the end of the row. Repeat this row.

### Chain stitch selvage on one edge

Row 1: Work as row 1, above.
Row 2: Knit to end.
   Repeat these two rows. The chain stitch selvage is formed at the beginning of row 1.

# Hems

A hem forms an edge on a knitted garment where a rib or knitted selvage, such as garter stitch or moss stitch, would not be suitable. A hem eliminates curling and allows the garment to hang correctly by adding weight to the bottom. Waistbands or cuffs can be created by threading a piece of elastic or ribbon through a knitted hem. A hem is made by working an extra piece of knitting along the bottom edge, which is then folded and sewn or knitted into place. The folded part of the hem should be worked in stockinette or another smooth stitch to avoid bulk, and should be worked on smaller needles than the main body of knitting.

- **Plain Hem** (below left)

To achieve a neat fold, create a turning ridge once the hem has reached the required depth. The ridge is formed by working one row opposite the rest. In stockinette stitch, this would mean working a row knitwise in place of a purl row.

- **Picot Hem** (below)

Eyelets create a decorative turning ridge. Work with an even number of stitches, and finish on the wrong side once the hem is the required depth. Next row: Knit two together, yarn over (k2tog, yo), repeat ending k2. Turn and continue in stockinette stitch.

## • Knit-in Hem

It is possible to knit the hem before the rest of the garment. Check that the hem is correct before continuing with the pattern, since any mistakes are difficult to rectify without unraveling the knitted piece.

### Step 1
Work as for a plain hem until both pieces, either side of the turning ridge, are the same length, ending with a wrong-side row. Leave the stitches on the needle with yarn attached.

### Step 2
Using a spare piece of the same yarn, and a needle of the same size, pick up one loop through the center of every stitch along the cast-on edge. Cut the yarn, leaving a small tail.

### Step 3
Turn the work, fold the hem and use a third needle to work across the row, knitting the two pieces together.

## • Picked-up Hem

You can create a vertical facing by picking up stitches along the edge and working them in the same way as for a horizontal hem. To do this, pick up the number of stitches required along the edge. Work until the hem is the correct depth, make the turning ridge and complete to match the first side of the hem. Then bind off and slipstitch (see page 64) into place.

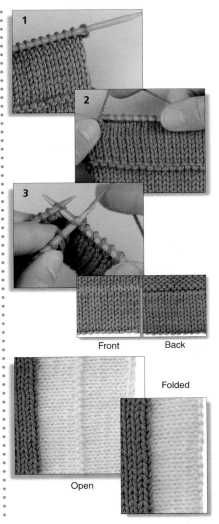

Front          Back

Folded

Open

# Tassels and Bobbles

Tassels are very easy to make and can brighten up a garment such as a scarf.

### Step 1
Wrap some yarn around a piece of cardboard that is the length of the tassel you want to make. About 10 wraps are used here.

### Step 2
Thread a piece of yarn through the top of the tassel between the yarn and the cardboard. Tie to secure, and leave a long end for sewing the tassel in place later.

### Step 3
Cut the yarn along the bottom edge of the cardboard.

### Step 4
Wrap a length of yarn around the tassel near the top, knot tightly, then repeat one or two times. Trim the tassel.

## • To make a sew-on bobble

### Step 1
Work a separate bobble on a slightly finer needle than that used for knitting. Cast on the required number of stitches (the more stitches, the larger the bobble). Often five or six stitches are sufficient. Work an uneven number of rows in either stockinette or garter stitch until the piece is the required length, ending with a right-side row.

### Step 2
Slip all the stitches used to make the bobble over the top of the last. Cut the knitting yarn approximately 8 inches (20 cm) from the needles, and pull it through the remaining knitted stitch.

### Step 3
Thread a knitter's sewing needle with the end of the yarn still attached to the bobble, and sew a running stitch around the outside edge of the bobble. Pull up tightly and secure.

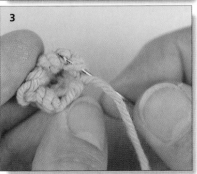

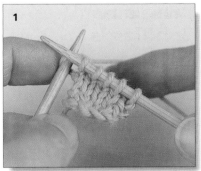

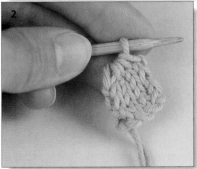

# Pompoms and Cords

Pompoms are very easy to make using a pompom maker or circles of cardboard.

### Step 1
Cut out two circles of cardboard about 1 inch (2.5 cm) larger than the pompom you want to make. Cut a small wedge out of each circle, then cut out a central 1 inch (2.5 cm) hole.

### Step 2
Holding the circles together and starting at the outer edge, wind the yarn around the circles until they are completely covered and the central hole is quite full.

Cut the yarn. If you are using a pompom maker and the central hole is too small to push the yarn through, thread a large yarn needle with two or three yarn ends, about 3 feet (1 m) long. Use the needle to thread the yarn through the center of the pompom maker.

### Step 3
Push the blade of a pair of scissors between the two circles and cut around the pompom.

### Step 4
Tie a piece of yarn around the center of the pompom as tightly as possible, between the cardboard layers. Remove the cardboard circles and trim the pompom to form a neat ball.

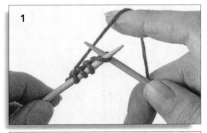

## • Knitting I-cord

I-cord is very easy to knit using double-pointed needles.

### Step 1
Cast on the required number of stitches and knit 1 row. Slide the stitches along the right needle from the left to the right tip. Transfer this needle to your left hand so that the working end of the yarn is coming from the bottom stitch on the needle.

### Step 2
Knit the next row, pulling the yarn tightly across the back of the stitches as you do so. Repeat this process until the cord is the required length. Cut the yarn, thread it through all the stitches and fasten securely.

## • Spool Knitting

Spool knitting creates a circular tube similar to that created by knitting a cord on double-pointed needles.

### Step 1
Thread the yarn through the center of the spool, with the tail end emerging from the bottom. Wrap the yarn around each peg or nail clockwise, pulling tightly.

### Step 2
Working each stitch separately, wrap the yarn around the back of the next peg, and transfer the existing wrapped stitch over the top with a blunt needle or small crochet hook. As you continue, the cord begins to emerge below from the center of the spool.

### Step 3
When the cord is the reguired length, bind off by moving the last stitch worked along to the next peg. Transfer the stitch over the top of it and repeat until one stitch remains. Cut the yarn and pull the final stitch through.

# Fringes

A fringe can add a wonderful finishing touch to the edges of a garment or knitted shawl. Fringing looks lovely when added to a collar, and can be embellished further by adding beads.

## • Knitted Fringe

This fringe is sewn on once the knitted piece is completed, and is worked in garter stitch.

### Step 1
Cast on the number of stitches that, when knitted, make approximately one-fifth the depth of the required fringe. Work in garter stitch until the band is the required length. Bind off the first four or five stitches.

### Step 2
Unravel the remaining stitches to create the fringe. This may be left as loops or trimmed.

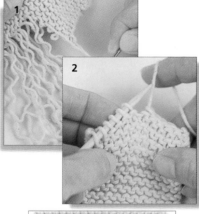

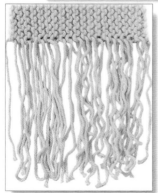

## • Using a Crochet Hook

This is a very simple fringe to make.

### Step 1
Cut lengths of yarn to double the length of the required fringe, plus a little more to allow for the knot. Fold one strand in half, push the crochet hook throught th edge of the knitting, catch the loop and draw it through.

### Step 2
Catch the two ends of the fringing and pull through the loop. As you pull, the knot will tighten.

## • Knotted Fringe

A knotted fringe is worked in the same way as a crochet-hook fringe and is subsequently knotted. Allow extra yarn for the knots. Divide every section of fringe in half, and knot each half of one together with half of the next fringe in line.

## • Beaded Fringe

A beaded fringe adds weight to the bottom edge of a piece and creates a sophisticated, "dressy" effect. Use either the crochet hook or knitted method. Thread a bead onto each strand of the fringe, and tie a knot below the bead to hold it in place.

# Knitted Flowers

Crochet flowers have traditionally been used to adorn garments and blankets, but knitted ones can look just as effective, especially when used on a very plain piece.

Flowers are knitted separately and then sewn onto a background, either singly or in groups to create effect of a bouquet. Think carefully about the yarns used to make the flowers. Fancy yarns, such as chenille and ribbon, work extremely well.

## • Basic Petal

This type of petal is perfect for making flowers with overlapping petals. For a larger petal, cast on more stitches (an uneven number) and work more rows.

**Step 1**
Cast on three stitches. Working in stockinette stitch, increase one stitch at each end on every right side row to nine stitches. Work six rows straight.

**Step 2**
Start to decrease each side of the petal by working as follows: slip one, knit one, pass slipped stitch over, knit to last two stitches, knit two together. Continue to decrease in this way on every alternate row to three stitches: slip one, knit two together, pass slip stitch over and fasten off.

## • Basic Knitted Flower

This flower is knitted in one piece and does not need to be sewn together once completed.

### Step 1
Cast on a multiple of 11 plus two stitches. (The more multiples you have, the more petals the flower will have.) Purl one row.

### Step 2
Next row: knit two*, knit one. Slip this stitch back onto the left needle. Pass the next eight stitches over the top of this stitch and off the needle. Take the yarn over the needle twice (pass the yarn forward and over twice to make two stitches), knit the first stitch again, then knit two stitches. Repeat from * to end.

### Step 3
Next row: purl one*, purl two together. Purl into the front of the first yarn over, then into the back of the second, purl one. Repeat from * to last stitch, purl one.

### Step 4
Next row: knit two together, repeat to end. Purl one row. Cut your yarn and thread tail into a yarn needle. Pass needle through remaining stitches and pull to tighten. Fasten off.

**TIP**

*Study flowers if you have the opportunity – many complex flower shapes can be made using a combination of the above patterns. For example, use the basic knitted flower pattern to create the center, and then attach petal shapes around the outside edge. Knit a larger basic petal shape in a shade of green or brown to make a leaf.*

# Using Beads

Knitting with beads can be done in a number of ways, but for all methods the beads are threaded onto the yarn before casting on. You may need to thread the beads onto the yarn in sections – too many prestrung beads can make knitting difficult and affect the gauge.

## • Placing a Bead Using a Slip Stitch

This is done using garter stitch or stockinette on the right side of the work. Beads can be placed every alternate stitch and every other row. The bead falls directly in front of the slipped stitch.

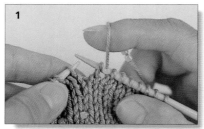

### Step 1
Work to where the bead is required. Slide the bead up the yarn. Bring the yarn forward between the needles with the bead to the front, and slip the next stitch purlwise.

### Step 2
Keep the bead as close to the knitting as possible, holding it in front of the slipped stitch with a finger or thumb if necessary, then take the yarn back between the needles leaving the yarn in front. Knit the next stitch firmly.

## • Placing a Bead Within a Stitch

Using this technique, the beads are
placed on the reverse of the work and
pushed through to the front. The bead is
held within the stitch and lies at a slight
angle on one side of it.

### On a knit row

**Step 1**
Work to where the bead is required.
Insert the right knitting needle into the
stitch knitwise. Slide the bead up the yarn
until it meets the work.

**Step 2**
Knit the stitch, pushing the bead through
the stitch so that it appears on the other
side of the work. Knit the next stitch
firmly.

### On a purl row

**Step 1**
Insert the right knitting needle into the
stitch purlwise and wrap the yarn around
it as if to purl. Slide the bead up the yarn
until the bead meets the work.

**Step 2**
Push the bead through the stitch to the
right side and complete the stitch.

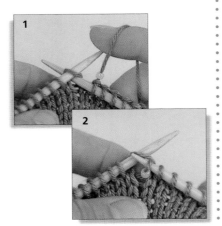

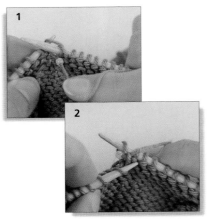

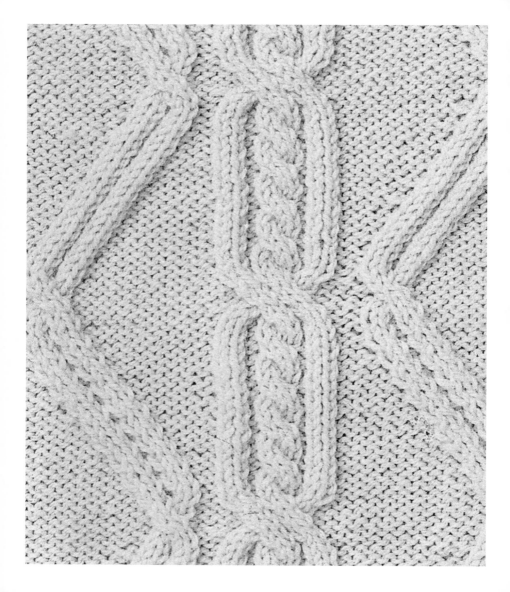

# Knitting
# Stitches

# How to Use Charts

Working from charts has many advantages, the main one being the immediacy with which the relationship between stitches and rows is illustrated. This makes understanding the construction of a stitch pattern and memorizing a repeat much easier. It's also an incentive to adapt existing stitches and invent new ones.

As the number of different symbols used in any one stitch pattern is small, they can be learned a few at a time as required. All the symbols have been chosen to be pictorial rather than abstract representations of a stitch or technique.

Abbreviations can be found on page 96.

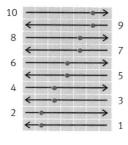

Chart A

**CHART A**

- Each square of the chart represents a stitch, and each row of squares represents a row of stitches.
- The numbers up the sides of the chart are row numbers, and therefore progress from the bottom to the top like the knitted sample.
- All rows that are numbered on the right-hand side of the chart are read from that side, and represent right-side rows.
- All rows that are numbered on the left-hand side of the chart are read from that side and represent wrong-side rows. It's useful to get into the habit of reading all charts in this way, and it's essential when working stitch patterns that are not symmetrical.

Thus, Chart A reads:

1st row: (right side) k5, p1, k1.

2nd row: p1, k1, p5 (worked from left to right).

3rd row: k4, p1, k2 (worked from right to left).

4th row: p2, k1, p4 and so on, reading right-side rows from the right and wrong-side rows from the left.

- If a stitch pattern is to be worked in the round with right-side facing, all rows are read from the right-hand side.

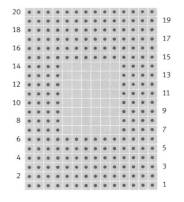

Chart Bi

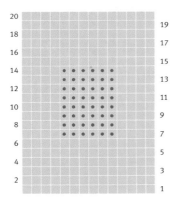

Chart Bii

## CHART B

Each symbol within a square indicates the way a stitch is worked. Initially, it may seem confusing that a blank square represents two stitches (knit on a right-side row, and purl on a wrong-side row) and that a dot represents two stitches (purl on a right-side row, and knit on a wrong-side row). But comparing a knitted sample with its chart reveals the logic of this immediately. The blank squares convey the appearance of the smooth side of the stitch as in stockinette, and the dotted squares convey the appearance of the rounded side of the stitch as in reverse stockinette (see charts and samples Bi and Bii). All that's needed to know whether a stitch is knit or purl is to know which side of the fabric is being worked.

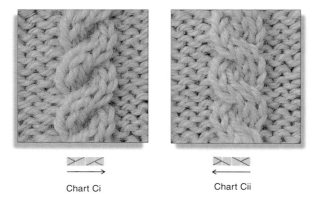

Chart Ci

Chart Cii

## CHART C

Cable symbols extend over the number of stitches involved in the cable cross, so the cable glossary runs from the smallest cables requiring only two stitches to those requiring nine stitches. As far as possible, the symbols are drawn to look like the resulting cable. In this collection cables are worked on right-side rows only, and so it helps to remember that diagonals that slope backward (i.e., toward the beginning of the row) have the cable needle held at the back of the work, and diagonals that slope forward (i.e., toward the end of the row) have the cable needle held at the front of the work. Thus, in Chart Ci the symbol represents sl (slip) 2 sts onto cable needle and hold at back, k2 then k2 from cable needle. In Chart Cii, the symbol represents sl 2 sts onto cable needle and hold at front, k2 then k2 from cable needle.

## CHARTS D AND E

To make some charts look more like the resulting cable stitches, additional lines have been drawn in. These are merely to help the eye distinguish between one group of stitches and another and do not affect the working of the stitches. In the same way, lines have been used to distinguish one area from another where symbols are very dense and might be difficult to follow. Any exceptional symbols are explained beside the relevant chart.

Chart D

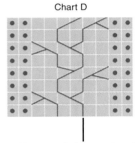

These verticals are not worked

Chart E

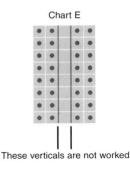

These verticals are not worked

## CHART F

A blocked-out square represents no stitch at all, for example, a stitch lost by decreasing and not compensated for with an increase. These blocked-out areas are not to be included in any stitch count, and any loss of vertical alignment of stitches in the chart must be ignored.

Thus, F shows a chart that begins with 5 sts, increases 2 sts on both rows 3 and 5, is worked over 9 sts on rows 6, 7 and 8 before decreasing 2 sts on both rows 9 and 11 to return to 5 sts on row 12.

Chart F

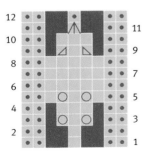

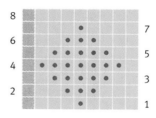

Chart G

Multiple of 8 sts plus 1

## CHART G

- The area of a chart that is unshaded and also has a square bracket underneath indicates a group of stitches forming a repeat.
- A shaded area indicates stitches that are worked at the beginning or end of a row to balance the repeat.
- The number of stitches required for the repeat is given as a "Multiple of... sts," and the number of end stitches as "plus..."
- In Chart G "Multiple of 8 sts plus 1" means cast on a number of stitches divisible by 8 and add 1 more.

## CHARTS H AND I

An unshaded area underlined by an H-shaped bracket indicates a panel or motif, and shaded areas indicate a notional number of stitches to the sides of the pattern area. In a panel all the rows of the chart are repeated. A motif may have an odd number of rows, and any number of "background" rows may be worked below and above.

Chart H

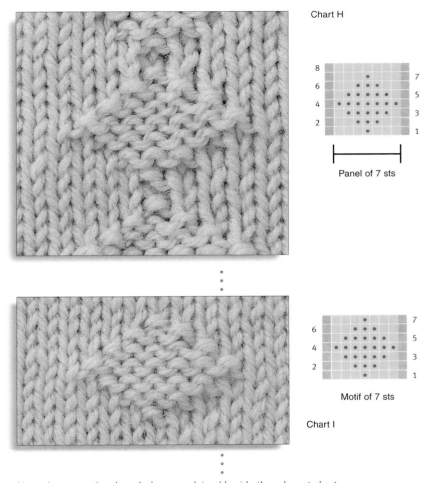

8
7
6
5
4
3
2
1

Panel of 7 sts

7
6
5
4
3
2
1

Motif of 7 sts

Chart I

Note: Any exceptional symbols are explained beside the relevant chart.

# Glossary of Symbols

## • Abbreviations

| | |
|---|---|
| Alt | Alternate. |
| K | Knit. |
| Psso | Pass slipped st(s) over. |
| P | Purl. |
| RS | Right side. |
| Skpo | Sl 1 st knitwise, k1, pass slipped st over. |
| Sl | Slip. |
| St(s) | Stitch(es). |
| Tbl | Through back of loop(s). |
| Tog | Together. |
| T2l | Twist 2 sts to left: taking needle behind work, k in back loop of 2nd st on left-hand needle, k in front of 1st st; sl both sts off tog. |
| T2r | Twist 2 sts to right; k2tog leaving sts on needle, insert right-hand needle between sts just worked and k 1st st again; sl both sts from needle. |
| WS | Wrong side. |
| Yo | Yarn forward and over needle to make a st. |

## • Knit and purl

K1 on right-side rows, p1 on wrong-side rows.

P1 on right-side rows, k1 on wrong-side rows.

K1 tbl on right-side rows, p1 tbl on wrong-side rows.

K1 tbl on wrong-side rows.

Sl 1 st purlwise, taking yarn behind work.

Sl 1 st purlwise, taking yarn in front of work.

Yarn forward and over needle to make a st.

Make a st by picking up strand in front of next st and k it through back loop

Make a st by picking up strand in front of next st and p it through back loop.

Increase 1 st by working k in front, then back of st.

Increase 1 st by working p in back, then front of st.

Increase 2 sts by working (k1, p1, k1) in st.

Increase 2 sts by working (k1 tbl, k1) in st then insert left-hand needle behind the vertical strand running downward between the 2 sts just worked and work this strand k1 tbl.

Multiple increase – method given beside chart.

K2tog on right-side rows, p2tog on wrong-side rows.

Skpo on right-side rows, p2 tog tbl on wrong-side rows.

P2tog on right-side rows, k2tog on wrong-side rows.

P2tog tbl on right-side rows.

K3tog.

K3tog tbl.

P3tog.

Sl 1 knitwise, k2tog, psso.

Sl 2 sts as if to work k2tog; k1, psso.

Cast off I st.

St left on right-hand needle after casting off.

Knot: (k1, p1, k1, p1, k1) in st to make 5 sts from I, then pass 2nd, 3rd, 4th and 5th sts, one at a time, over 1st st.

Large knot: (k1, p1, k1, p1, k1, p1, k1) in st to make 7 sts from 1, pass 2nd, 3rd, 4th, 5th, 6th and 7th sts, one at a time, over 1st st.

Small bobble: (k1, p1, k1, p1, k1) in st to make 5 sts from 1, turn, p5, turn; pass 2nd, 3rd, 4th and 5th sts, one at a time, over 1st st then k in back of this st.

Large bobble: (k1, p1, k1, p1, k1) in st to make 5 sts from 1, turn, p5, turn, k5, turn, p5, turn; pass 2nd, 3rd, 4th and 5th sts over 1st st then k in back of this st.

Purl bobble: (p in front, back, front, back, front) of st to make 5 sts from 1, turn, k5, turn, p5, turn, k5, turn; pass 2nd, 3rd, 4th and 5th sts, one at a time, over 1st st then k in back of this st.

Wide bobble (k2, turn, p2, turn) twice (k next st tog with corresponding st of 1st row of bobble) twice.

Sl 3 sts onto cable needle, wind yarn counterclockwise around base of sts 8 times, ending with yarn at back of work, sl sts onto right-hand needle.

Sl 4 sts onto cable needle, wind yarn counterclockwise around base of sts 4 times, ending with yarn at back of work, sl sts onto right-hand needle.

Sl 5 sts onto cable needle, wind yarn counterclockwise around base of sts 4 times, ending with yarn at back of work, sl sts on to right-hand needle.

Sl 6 sts onto cable needle, wind yarn counterclockwise around base of sts 4 times, ending with yarn at back of work, sl sts onto right-hand needle.

Sl 10 sts onto cable needle, wind yarn counterclockwise around base of sts 4 times, ending with yarn at back of work, sl sts onto right-hand needle.

No stitch.

Twist 2 sts to right: k2tog, leaving sts on needle, insert right-hand needle between sts just worked and k 1st st again; sl both sts off tog.

Twist 2 sts to left: taking needle behind work, k in back loop of 2nd st on left-hand needle, k both sts tog tbl; sl both sts off tog.

Purl twist to right: taking needle to front of work, k 2nd st on left-hand needle, p 1st st; sl both sts off tog.

Purl twist to left: taking needle behind work, p in back of 2nd st on left-hand needle, k in front of 1st st; sl both sts off tog.

Twist 3 sts; taking needle to front of work, k 3rd st on left-hand needle, then 2nd st, then 1st st; sl all sts off tog.

## • Cables

Sl 1 st onto cable needle and hold at back, k1 then k1 from cable needle.

Sl 1 st onto cable needle and hold at front, k1 then k1 from cable needle.

Sl 1 st onto cable needle and hold at back, k1 then p1 from cable needle.

Sl 1 st onto cable needle and hold at front, p1 then k1 from cable needle.

Sl 2 sts onto cable needle and hold at back, k1 then k2 from cable needle.

Sl 1 st onto cable needle and hold at front, k2 then k1 from cable needle.

Sl 2 sts onto cable needle and hold at back, k1 then p2 from cable needle.

Sl 1 st onto cable needle and hold at front, p2 then k1 from cable needle.

Sl 2 sts onto cable needle and hold at back, k1, sl last st from cable neddle back onto left-hand needle and p this st, then k1from cable needle.

Sl 1 st onto cable needle and hold at front, k1, p1 then k1 from cable needle.

Sl 1 st onto cable needle and hold at back,k2, then k1 from cable needle.

Sl 1 st onto cable needle and hold at front, k1, p1 then k1 from cable needle.

Sl 1 st onto cable needle and hold at back, k2 then p1 from cable needle.

Sl 2 sts onto cable needle and hold at front, p1 then k2 from cable needle.

Sl 1 st onto cable needle and hold at back, t2r then p1 from cable needle.

Sl 2 sts onto cable needle and hold at front, p1 then t2r from cable needle.

Sl 2 sts onto cable needle and hold at back, k2 then k2 from cable needle.

Sl 2 sts onto cable needle and hold at front, k2 then k2 from cable needle.

Sl 2 sts onto cable needle and hold at back, k2 then p2 from cable needle.

Sl 2 sts onto cable needle and hold at front, p2 then k2 from cable needle.

Sl 1 st onto cable needle and hold at back, k3 then p1 from cable needle.

Sl 3 sts onto cable needle and hold at front, p1 then k3 from cable needle.

Sl 3 sts onto cable needle and hold at back, k2, sl last st from cable needle back onto left-hand needle and k this st then k2 from cable needle.

Sl 2 sts onto 1st cable needle and hold at front, sl 1 st onto 2nd cable needle and hold at back, k2; k1 from 2nd cable needle then k2 from 1st cable needle.

Sl 3 sts onto cable needle and hold at back, k2, sl last st from cable needle back onto left-hand needle and p this st then k2 from cable needle.

Sl 2 sts onto 1st cable needle and hold at front, sl 1 st onto 2nd cable needle and hold at back, k2; p1 from 2nd cable needle then k2 from 1st cable needle.

Sl 1 st onto 1st cable needle and hold at front, sl 3 sts onto 2nd cable needle and hold at back, k1; p3 from 2nd cable needle then k1 from 1st cable needle.

Sl 2 sts onto cable needle and hold at back, k3 then p2 from cable needle.

Sl 3 sts onto cable needle and hold at front, p2 then k3 from cable needle.

Sl 1 st onto cable needle and hold at back, t2r, t2l then k1 from cable needle.

Sl 4 sts onto cable needle and hold at front, k1 then t2r, t2l from cable needle.

Sl 1 st onto cable needle  and hold at back, t2r, t2l then p1 from cable needle.

Sl 4 sts onto cable needle  and hold at front, p1 then t2r, t2l from cable needle.

Sl 1 st onto cable needle  and hold at back, t2l, t2r then p1 from cable needle.

Sl 4 sts onto cable needle  and hold at front, p1 then t2l, t2r from cable needle.

Sl 3 sts onto cable 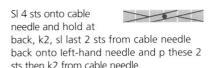 needle and hold at back, k3 then k3 from cable needle.

Sl 3 sts onto cable needle and hold at front, k3 then k3 from cable needle.

Sl 4 sts onto cable  needle and hold at back, k2, sl last 2 sts from cable needle back onto left-hand needle and p these 2 sts then k2 from cable needle.

Sl 2 sts onto 1st cable needle and hold at front, sl 2 sts onto 2nd cable needle and hold at back, k2; p2 from 2nd cable needle then k2 from 1st cable needle.

Sl 4 sts onto cable needle and hold at back, k3, sl last st from cable needle back onto left-hand needle and k this st then k3 from cable needle.

Sl 4 sts onto cable needle and hold at back, k3, sl last st from cable needle back onto left-hand needle and p this st then k3 from cable needle.

Sl 4 sts onto cable needle and hold at back, k4 then k4 from cable needle.

Sl 4 sts onto cable needle and hold at front, k4 then k4 from cable needle.

Sl 5 sts onto cable needle and hold at back, k4 then k5 from cable needle.

Sl 4 sts onto cable needle and hold at back, k5 then k4 from cable needle.

# Knit and Purl stitches

# Popular Knit and Purl Stitches

These knit and purl stitches can be used to make a range of items, from cushions and traditional sweaters to fashion designs in crisp textures and subtle brocades – the possibilities are endless.

## Seed Stitch

With an odd number of stitches, seed stitch is a one-row pattern. On every row simply knit the first stitch, then purl one, knit one to the end of the row. On an even number of stitches, seed stitch is a two-row pattern.

A quick way to represent knit and purl is by a chart (see *How to use charts* on pages 90–95). You can start seed stitch with either a knit or a purl stitch.

When working on an even number of stitches, if the first stitch of the first row is knit, the first stitch of the second row will be purl.

Multiple of 2 sts plus 1

Multiple of 2 sts plus 1

Multiple of 2 sts plus 2

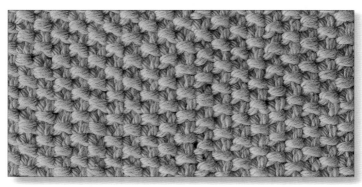

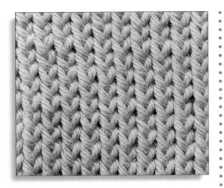

## Crossed Stockinette Stitch

To work crossed stockinette stitch, knit into the back of each stitch on right-side rows, and purl into the back of each stitch on wrong-side rows.

## Barred Stockinette Stitch

For barred stockinette, purl on wrong-side rows, and knit and slip alternately on right-side rows, holding the yarn in front.

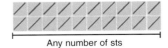

Any number of sts

Multiple of 2 sts plus 1

## 2 and 3 Welting

Welting patterns can be worked on any number of stitches, odd or even, and with any combination of rows of reverse stockinette stitch and stockinette stitch. This fabric spreads in width and contracts vertically.

## Little Blocks

Patterns of alternating blocks of stockinette stitch and reverse stockinette stitch can be worked over any combination of stitches and rows. Block patterns have a similar gauge to that of stockinette stitch, so the little blocks here appear square even though there are more rows than stitches to each block.

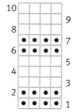

Shown over 4 sts

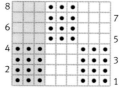

Multiple of 6 sts plus 3

## Broken Blocks

Adding a garter ridge to the stockinette stitch blocks makes this pattern look more exciting than plain blocks, yet it's very easy to work.

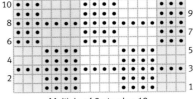

Multiple of 8 sts plus 10

## Double Seed Stitch

Double seed stitch – also called Irish moss – is always a four-row pattern, but it can be worked over an odd or an even number of stitches, starting knit or purl as for seed stitch. The chart shows double seed stitch beginning with purl, as this holds the corner of knitting more neatly. If double seed stitch is to be used after knit one, purl one rib (see page 156), then start with a knit stitch, as in the third row of the chart. Double moss is an extremely useful stitch because the row gauge is similar to that of stockinette stitch, which makes it ideal for creating textured motifs on a stockinette stitch background.

Multiple of 2 sts plus 1

## Tiny Double Seed Diamonds

This stitch shows the smallest possible double seed stitch diamonds on stockinette stitch. Use it as an all-over pattern, or work just three or four repeats for a textured panel.

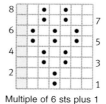

Multiple of 6 sts plus 1

## Cornish Lattice

This stitch pattern is based on purl garter stitch and stockinette, which makes it easy to work.

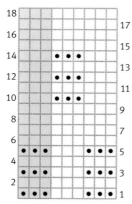

Multiple of 6 sts plus 3

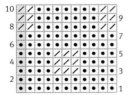

## Garter Diamonds

Although the large repeat makes this pattern look complicated, it's easy to work because it's made with knit and purl stitches on right-side rows, and every wrong-side row is just purl.

## Twisted Little Check

Working the stockinette stitch squares through the back of the loops gives a lovely definition to the blocks.

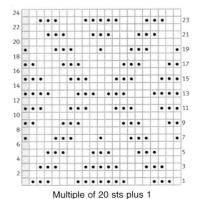

Multiple of 20 sts plus 1

Multiple of 10 sts plus 1

## Twisted Diagonal

You could work the stockinette stitch part of this pattern without twisting the stitches, but the result would be less well-defined diagonals. For a diagonal running to the right, reverse the chart.

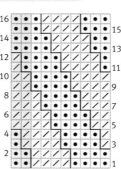

Multiple of 8 sts plus 1

## Twisted Chevron

When diagonals are worked in alternate directions, they meet to make chevrons. Working stitches through the back of the loops makes the chevrons appear taller and more elegant.

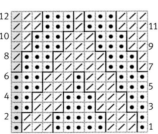

Multiple of 12 sts plus 1

## Twisted Square Check

See how the small blocks of stitches, which are worked through the back of the loops, contrast with the stockinette stitch outlining the blocks.

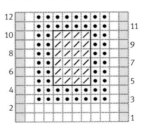

Multiple of 10 sts plus 2

## Double Seed Stitch Star

This star can be used as a single motif, scattered on a stockinette stitch background or repeated in blocks. If you're planning to use it as a repeat pattern, chart it out fully to make sure that you have allowed enough extra stockinette stitch background stitches between the stars.

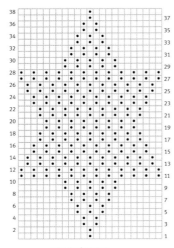

Motif of 23 sts

## Double Seed Stitch Heart

This heart motif can be used in the same way as the star or combined with other stitch patterns. It's very easy to make this motif larger – simply copy this design onto graph paper, then add more pairs of dots for purl stitches evenly all around the motif until the heart is the size you want.

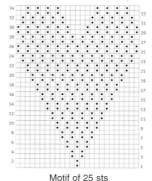

Motif of 25 sts

## Linen Stitch

This densely woven fabric is made by slipping stitches on both right- and wrong-side rows. Remember to bring the yarn forward before slipping a stitch on right-side rows, and to take the yarn back before slipping a stitch on wrong-side rows, so that the strands always appear on the right side of the work.

Multiple of 2 sts plus 3

# Easy Knit and Purl Stitches

You can alternate knit and purl and you get the simplest texture stitches. Group the knits and purls geometrically to make blocks, diagonals, chevrons and diamonds, or put them together more freely to create motifs.

## Easy Stitch 1

Multiple of 4 sts plus 1.
1st row: (right side) k.
2nd row: p.
3rd row: * k1, p3; repeat from * to last st, k1.
4th row: p.
Repeat rows 1–4.

## Easy Stitch 2

Multiple of 5 sts plus 2.
1st row: (right side) * k2, p3; repeat from * to last 2 sts, k2.
2nd row: p.
Repeat rows 1 and 2.

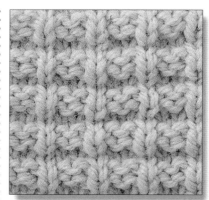

## Easy Stitch 3

Multiple of 6 sts plus 1.
This stitch is reversible.
1st row: (right side) * p1, k5; repeat from * to last st, p1.
2nd row: p1, k5, p1; repeat from * to end.
Repeat rows 1 and 2.

## Easy Stitch 4

Multiple of 3 sts plus 1.
1st row: (right side) * k1, p2; repeat from * to last st, k1.
2nd row: p1, * k2, p1; repeat from * to end.
3rd row: k.
4th row: p.
Repeat rows 1–4.

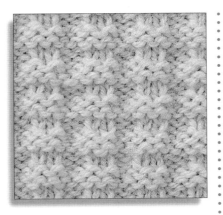

## Easy Stitch 5

Multiple of 4 sts plus 2.
1st row: (right side) p.
2nd row: k.
3rd row: * k2, p2; repeat from * to last 2 sts, k2.
4th row: p2, k2, p2; repeat from * to end.
Repeat rows 1–4.

## Easy Stitch 6

Multiple of 4 sts plus 1.
1st row: (right side) * k1, p3; repeat from * to last st, k1.
2nd row: p.
3rd row: * p2, k1, p1; repeat from * to last st, p1.
4th row: p.
Repeat rows 1–4.

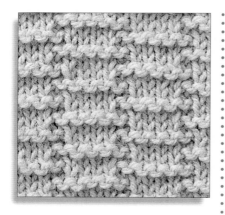

## Easy Stitch 7

Multiple of 10 sts plus 6.
1st row: (right side) * p6, k4; repeat from * to last 6 sts, p6.
2nd row: p.
3rd row: * p1, k4, p5; repeat from * to last 6 sts, p1, k4, p1.
4th row: p.
Repeat rows 1–4.

## Easy Stitch 8

Multiple of 8 sts plus 5.
1st row: (right side) * p2, k1, p2, k3; repeat from * to last 5 sts, p2, k1, p2.
2nd row: k5, * k1, p1, k6; repeat from * to end.
Repeat rows 1 and 2.

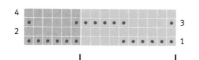

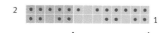

## Easy Stitch 9

Multiple of 6 sts plus 3.
This stitch is reversible.
1st row: (right side) * p1, k1; repeat from * to last st, p1.
2nd row: k3, * p3, k3; repeat from * to end.
Repeat rows 1 and 2.

## Easy Stitch 10

Multiple of 6 sts plus 3.
1st and 3rd rows: (right side) * k3, p1, k1, p1; repeat from * to last 3 sts, k3.
2nd row: p3, k3, p3; repeat from * to end.
4th row: p.
5th and 7th rows: * p1, k1, p1, k3; repeat from * to last 3 sts, p1, k1, p1.
6th row: k3, * p3, k3; repeat from * to end.
8th row: p.
Repeat rows 1–8.

## Easy Stitch 11

Multiple of 2 sts plus 1.
1st and 3rd rows: (right side) k.
2nd and 4th rows: p.
5th row: * k1, p1; repeat from * to last st, k1.
6th row: p1, * k1, p1; repeat from * to end.
Repeat rows 1–6.

## Easy Stitch 12

Multiple of 6 sts plus 4.
1st and 3rd rows: (right side) * k1, p2, k3; repeat from * to last 4 sts, k1, p2, k1.
2nd and alt rows: p.
5th and 7th rows: * k4, p2; repeat from * to last 4 sts, k4.
8th row: p.
Repeat rows 1–8.

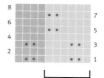

## Easy Stitch 13

Multiple of 8 sts plus 2.
1st row: (right side) * k2, p6; repeat from * to last 2 sts, k2.
2nd row: p2, * k6, p2; repeat from * to end.
3rd row: k
4th row: k2, * k2, p2, k4; repeat from * to end.
5th row: * p4, k2, p2; repeat from * to last 2 sts, p2.
6th row: p.
Repeat rows 1-6.

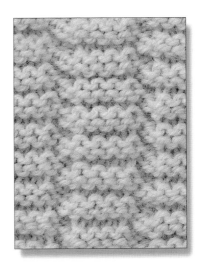

## Easy Stitch 14

Multiple of 12 sts plus 8.
1st row: (right side) * p8, k4; repeat from * to last 8 sts, p8.
2nd row: k8, * p4, k8; repeat from * to end.
3rd row: * p2, k4, p6; repeat from * to last 8 sts, p2, k4, p2.
4th row: k2, p4, k2, * k6, p4, k2; repeat from * to end.
Repeat rows 1–4.

## Easy Stitch 15

Multiple of 8 sts plus 4.
This stitch is reversible.
1st row: (right side) * k4, p4; repeat from
* to last 4 sts, k4.
2nd and alt rows: k all k sts and p all p
sts as they appear.
3rd row: p.
5th row: as 1st row.
7th row: k.
8th row: as 2nd row.
Repeat rows 1–8.

## Easy Stitch 16

Multiple of 6 sts plus 3.

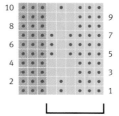

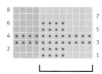

## Easy Stitch 17

Multiple of 12 sts plus 6.

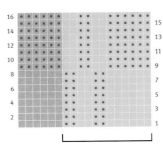

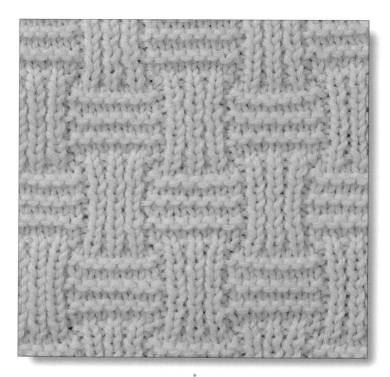

## Easy Stitch 18

Multiple of 14 sts plus 7.

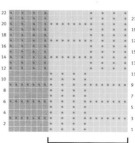

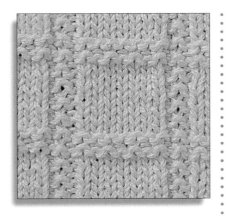

# Easy Stitch 19

Multiple of 10 sts plus 1.

# Easy Stitch 20

Multiple of 12 sts plus 1.

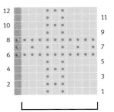

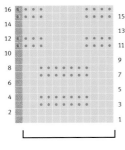

## Easy Stitch 21

Multiple of 10 sts plus 3.

## Easy Stitch 22

Multiple of 6 sts plus 2.

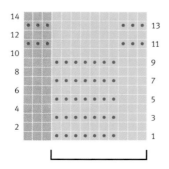

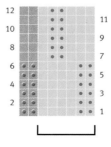

# Medium Knit and Purl Stitches

Knit and purl patterns can be repeated to make an all-over design or used in panels with simple stitches between.

## Medium Stitch 1

Multiple of 6 sts plus 3.
1st row: (right side) * p1, k1, p4; repeat from * to last 3 sts, p1, k1, p1.
2nd row: k1, p1, k1, * p3, k1, p1, k1; repeat from * to end.
3rd row: * p3, k3; repeat from * to last 3 sts, p3.
4th row: k1, p1, k1, * p3, k1, p1, k1; repeat from * to end.
Repeat rows 1–4.

## Medium Stitch 2

Multiple of 4 sts plus 3.
1st row: (right side) * p1, k1, p2; repeat from * to last 3 sts, p1, k1, p1.
2nd row: k1, p1, k1, * k2, p1, k1; repeat from * to end.
3rd row: p1, k1; repeat to last st, p1.
4th row: k1, p1, k1; repeat to end.
5th row: p3, k1; repeat to last 3 sts, p3.
6th row: k3, p1, k3; repeat to end.
7th row: as 3rd row
8th row: as 4th row.
Repeat rows 1–8.

## Medium Stitch 3

Multiple of 8 sts plus 1.
1st, 3rd, 5th and 7th rows: (right side) *
k2, p1, k3, p1, k1; repeat from * to last
st, k1.
2nd, 4th and 6th rows: p1, * p1, k5, p2;
repeat from * to end.
8th and 10th rows: k1, * k2, p3, k3;
repeat from * to
end.
9th and 11th rows:
k2, p1, k3, p1, k1;
repeat * to last st, k1.
12th row: as 8th row.
Repeat rows 1–12.

## Medium Stitch 4

Multiple of 11 sts.
1st row: (right side) * p3, (k1, p3) twice;
repeat from * to end.
2nd row: * k3, (p1, k3) twice; repeat
from *
to end.
3rd row: k.
4th row: * k5, p1, k5; repeat from * to
end.
5th row: p5, k1, p5; repeat to end.
6th row: p.
Repeat rows 1–6.

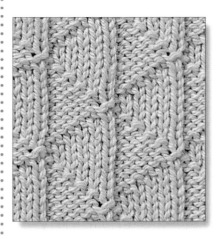

## Medium Stitch 5

Multiple of 9 sts plus 2.
1st row: (right side) * k2, p2, k3, p2;
repeat * to last 2 sts, k2.
2nd row: p.
3rd row: * k2, p7; repeat from * to last 2
sts, k2.
4th row: p.
Repeat rows 1–4.

## Medium Stitch 6

Multiple of 12 sts.

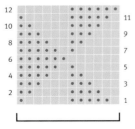

## Medium Stitch 7

Multiple of 12 sts.

## Medium Stitch 8

Multiple of 5 sts plus 1.

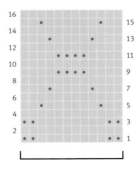

## Medium Stitch 9

Multiple of 14 sts plus 1.

## Medium Stitch 10

Multiple of 12 sts.

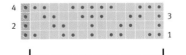

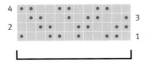

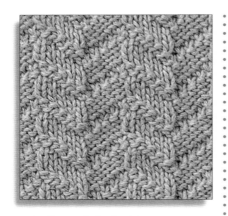

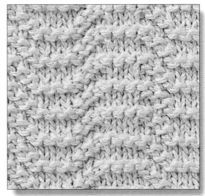

## Medium Stitch 11

Multiple of 10 sts.

## Medium Stitch 12

Multiple of 12 sts plus 1.

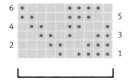

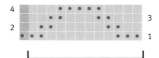

## Medium Stitch 13

Multiple of 10 sts plus 1.

## Medium Stitch 14

Multiple of 12 sts.

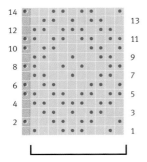

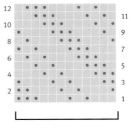

## Medium Stitch 15

Multiple of 10 sts plus 1.

## Medium Stitch 16

Multiple of 8 sts plus 5.

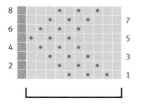

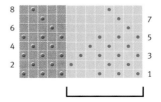

## Medium Stitch 17

Multiple of 10 sts plus 5.

## Medium Stitch 18

Multiple of 8 sts plus 1.

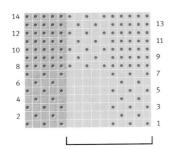

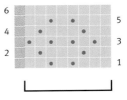

## Medium Stitch 19

Multiple of 14 sts plus 1.

## Medium Stitch 20

Multiple of 10 sts.

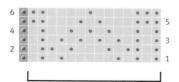

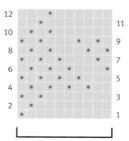

## Medium Stitch 21

Multiple of 6 sts plus 1.

## Medium Stitch 22

Multiple of 8 sts plus 1.

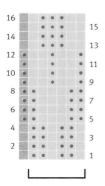

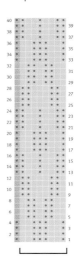

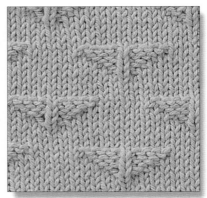

## Medium Stitch 23

Multiple of 16 sts.

## Medium Stitch 24

Multiple of 14 sts plus 1.

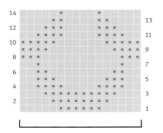

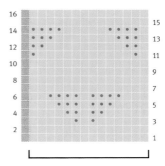

## Medium Stitch 25

Multiple of 12 sts. This stitch is reversible.

## Medium Stitch 26

Multiple of 10 sts plus 1.

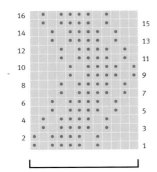

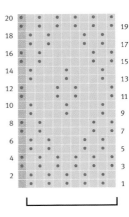

## Medium Stitch 27

Multiple of 10 sts.

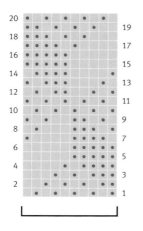

## Medium Stitch 28

Multiple of 18 sts plus 2.

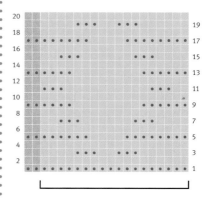

## Medium Stitch 29

Multiple of 16 sts plus 1.

## Medium Stitch 30

Multiple of 10 sts plus 1.

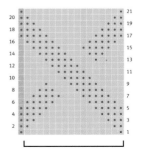

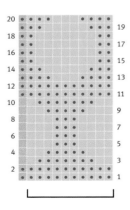

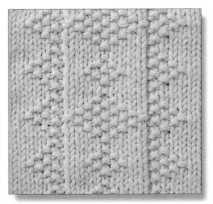

## Medium Stitch 31

Multiple of 22 sts plus 1.

## Medium Stitch 32

Panel of 19 sts.

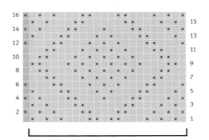

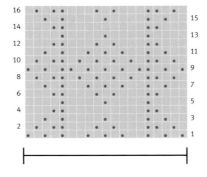

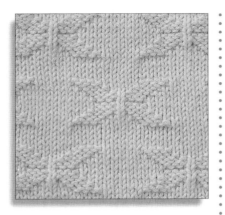

## Medium Stitch 33

Multiple of 18 sts plus 1.

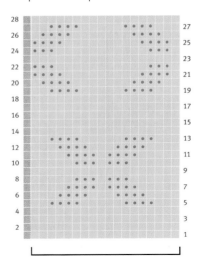

## Medium Stitch 34

Multiple of 16 sts plus 1.

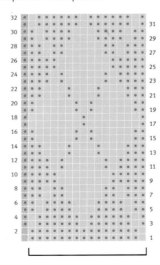

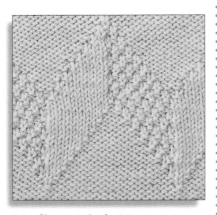

## Medium Stitch 35

Multiple of 18 sts.

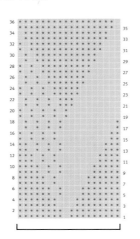

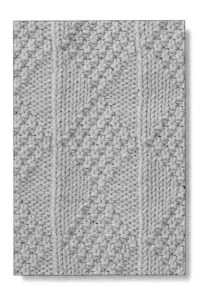

## Medium Stitch 36

Multiple of 12 sts. This stitch is reversible.

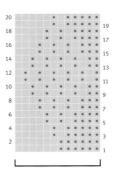

## Medium Stitch 37

Multiple of 20 sts plus 10.

## Medium Stitch 38

Multiple of 9 sts.

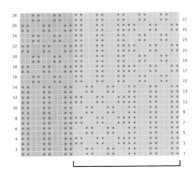

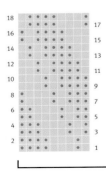

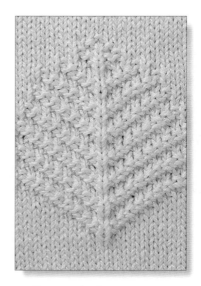

## Medium Stitch 39

Multiple of
20 sts plus 1.

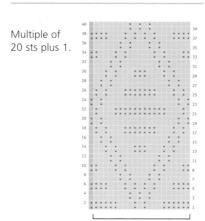

## Medium Stitch 40

Motif of
19 sts.

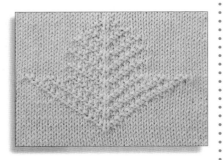

## Medium Stitch 41

Motif of 31 sts.

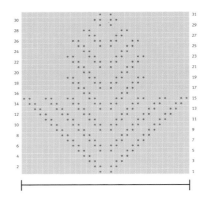

## Medium Stitch 42

Motif of 13 sts.

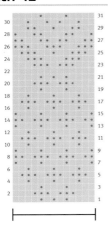

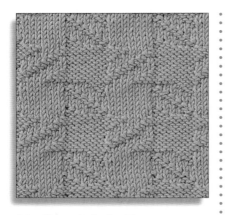

## Medium Stitch 43

Multiple of 14 sts plus 7.

## Medium Stitch 44

Multiple of 16 sts plus 4.

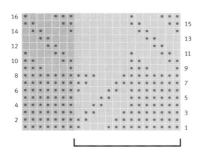

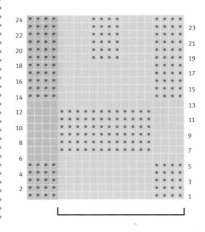

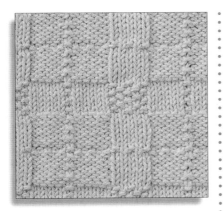

## Medium Stitch 45

Multiple of 16 sts plus 5.

## Medium Stitch 46

Multiple of 24 sts.

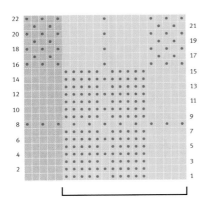

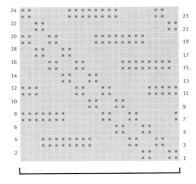

# Difficult Knit and Purl Stitches

You can add interest to knit and purl patterns by knitting into the back of the loops or slipping stitches.

## Difficult Stitch 1

Multiple of 30 sts plus 1.

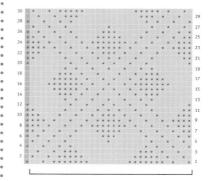

# Difficult Stitch 2

Motif of 61 sets.

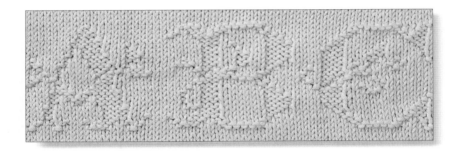

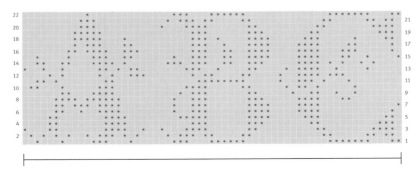

## Difficult Stitch 3

Multiple of 54 sts plus 1.

# Rib Stitches

# Easy Rib Stitches

Simple ribs are made up of combinations of knit and purl stitches that form verticals. These pull the knitting in across the width.

The knit stitches are raised and the purl stitches sink down. The resulting elasticity makes ribs very suitable for edgings and cuffs. If ribbed garments are designed to fit closely, choice of yarn is important. Wool, for example, will make a springy, stretchy rib, while cotton ribs will lie flat. In the wrong yarn, a skinny rib sweater just won't cling.

Ribs are usually worked on needles one, two, or more sizes smaller than for other stitches. The smaller the needle size, the more the rib will contract. Interesting patterns can be made by combining simple rib with cable, lace and twist stitches.

Measuring the length of a piece of ribbing can be difficult, since this measurement will vary depending on whether the knitting is stretched or contracted widthwise. In the end, it's best to measure ribs half-stretched unless the instructions state otherwise. The following is a selection of easy rib stitches.

## Single Rib

For this basic rib (also called Knit-one, purl-one Rib), alternate knit and purl stitches are worked above each other.

### Step 1
Over an even number of stitches repeat k1, p1 to the end of the row. The second row is the same.

### Step 2
Over an odd number of stitches, begin k1, then p1, k1 to the end. On alternate rows begin p1, then k1, p1 to the end.

Multiple of 2
sts plus 1

# Double Rib

Knit-two, purl-two rib makes an elastic fabric with strongly defined ridges and furrows. This rib can be worked on a number of stitches divisible by four – repeat k2, p2 along each row. To balance each end, work on a number of stitches divisible by four, plus two as follows:

### Step 1
The first row begins k2 and is followed by p2, k2 repeated to the end.

### Step 2
The second row begins p2, followed by k2, p2 to the end.

# Broken Rib

This variation on double rib does not pull in (see page 159).
Purling the wrong-side rows reduces the elasticity of the rib and produces an attractive texture.

 Multiple of 2 sts plus 1

## Single Twisted Rib

This well-defined rib has the knit stitches on the right side and the purl stitches on the wrong side worked through the back of the loop.

Multiple of 2
sts plus 1

## Knit Two, Purl Two Rib

Also known as the "double rib" or "two-and-two rib," this classic stitch is the same on both sides.

## Broken Double Rib

Purling wrong-side rows turns k2, p2 into a firm fabric with verticals of stockinette stitch and garter stitch.

Multiple of 4
sts plus 2

Multiple of 4
sts plus 2

## Bamboo Rib

Interrupting k2, p2 rib with small bands of welting makes an interesting variation on a familiar theme.

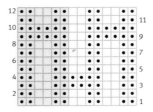

Multiple of 8 sts plus 6

## Diagonal Knit Two, Purl Two Rib

Moving k2, p2 ribs along one stitch on alternate rows produces well-defined diagonals.

Multiple of 4 sts

## Wide Rib

A wide rib can comprise any number of stitches. This one combines six of the stockinette stitch with two of the reverse stockinette stitch.

Multiple of 8
sts plus 2

## Stocking Heel Rib

This ribbed stitch is used to reinforce sock and stocking heels.

Multiple of 2
sts plus 1

## Seed and Slip Stitch Rib

Seed stitch panels make this slip stitch rib extra firm and substantial.

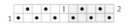

Multiple of 6 sts plus 5

## Crossed Rib

Although it looks like a twisted rib, this effect is achieved by taking a slipped stitch over an increase.

Multiple of 3 sts plus 1

 Sl 1 st knitwise, k in front and back of next st, psso.

## Fisherman's Rib

Knitting alternate stitches in the row below (see also page 157) is the secret of this deep, soft rib. Both sides look the same.

Multiple of 2 sts plus 3

After working row 1, repeat only rows 2 and 3

   K in the row below

## Brioche Rib

This rib looks similar to fisherman's rib, but is made quite differently (see page 157).

Yo, sl1 st purlwise, take yarn over needle.

K tog the sl st and the yo.

Multiple of 2 sts plus 3

# Cable Stitches

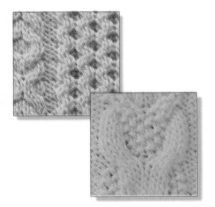

# Popular Cable Stitches

Cable stitches look like twisted ropes, interwoven plaits and criss-cross trellises. They may look complex, but they simply involve working stitches or groups of stitches out of sequence.

Cables are usually worked in stocking stitch on a plain or textured background but they look particularly rich when they themselves are textured.

They can be knitted, purled or textured as given in the pattern instructions. Once you have mastered the techniques for basic four-stitch cables, you will be able to tackle any of the stitches in this section. The basic four-stitch cables are explained below.

## Back Knit Cable

This four-stitch cable crosses at the back, and all the stitches are knitted.

**Step 1**
Slip the first two stitches onto cable needle and hold at the back of the work, then knit the next two stitches from the left needle.

**Step 2**
Knit the two stitches from the cable needle.

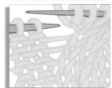

## Front Cable

For the front cable, all the stitches are knitted, but this four-stitch cable crosses at the front.

**Step 1**
Slip the first two stitches onto cable needle and hold at the front of the work, then knit the next two stitches from the left needle.

**Step 2**
Knit the two stitches from the cable needle.

## Back Purl Cable

Here's how to work a four-stitch cable with knit stitches moving to the right on a purl background – called c4bp.

### Step 1
Slip the first two stitches onto a cable needle and hold at the back of the work, then knit the next two stitches from the left needle.

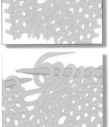

### Step 2
Purl the two stitches from the cable needle.

## Front Purl Cable

Here's how to work a four-stitch cable with knit stitches making a diagonal to the left on a purl background.

### Step 1
Slip the first two stitches onto a cable needle and hold at the front of the work, then purl the next two stitches from the left needle.

### Step 2
Knit the two stitches from the cable needle.

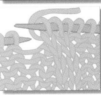

## Plaits and Ropes

Little cables worked over four rows are
fine on their own, but are especially good
for slipping in between bigger panels.
Here they are used with eight-row plaits.

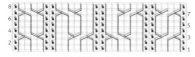

Multiple of 28 sts

## Oxo and Honeycomb

The center panel of honeycomb cable has
a repeat of eight stitches, so you could
work it over any multiple of eight to
make it wider or narrower.

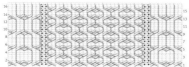

Panel of 44 sts

## Little Cable Ribs

Two-stitch crosses are often twisted, but
the smooth effect created by true cabling
is worth the extra work, as this pattern
shows. You could make the spiral wider
by adding any multiple of two stitches.

Multiple of 13 sts plus 6

## Cable Check

The easy three-over-three cables at the top of each block make this simple pattern of knit, and purl blocks look more complicated than it really is.

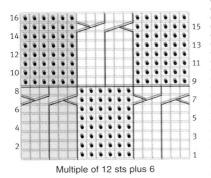

Multiple of 12 sts plus 6

## Cable Knot Rib

Here a six-stitch-wide cable alternates with a two-stitch rib. The pattern looks very complex, but it's easy to do.

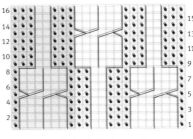

Multiple of 14 sts plus 8

## Plait and Rib

If you'd like a fatter plait, try working over twelve stitches, cabling four over four each time.

## Deckle Edge

Two-over-two cables along the edge of stockinette stitch panels contrast effectively with narrow bands of garter stitch. All wrong-side rows are purled.

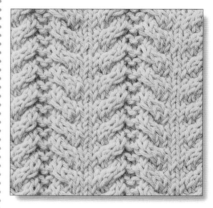

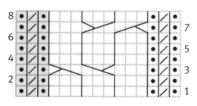

Multiple of 12 sts plus 3

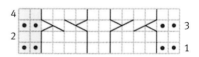

Multiple of 12 sts plus 2

# Two-textured Zigzag

This pattern is a good one for getting used to knit and purl cables, because the purl stitch always fits into the double seed stitch. To reverse the zigzag, start the chart on the 11th row.

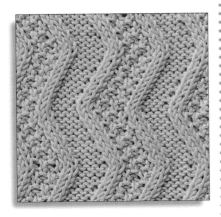

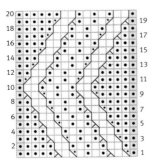

Multiple of 14 sts plus 2

# Textured Cable

Seed stitch is the texture used in this six-stitch cable, but k1, p1 rib could be substituted, with the knit stitches worked through the back of the loops.

Multiple of 16 sts plus 10

Sl 3 sts onto cable needle and hold at front, k3, then k1, p1, k1 from cable needle.

Sl 3 sts onto cable needle and hold at front, k1, p1, k1, then k3 from cable needle.

## Leaf Cable

These cabled leaves are used here for an all-over pattern, but they could also be combined with other cable stitches.

## Horseshoe Trellis

Extra cables springing out of the background add interest to an all-over trellis pattern.

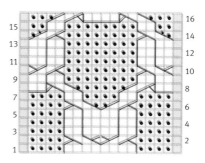

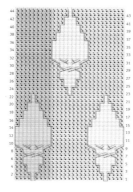

Multiple of 18 sts plus 9

Multiple of 16 sts plus 2

## Ribbed Rope Cable

Using crossed stitches gives this enclosed rope cable lots of character.

## Tulip Cable

One-over-one cables and stitches crossed by working through the back of the loop form stylized flowers.

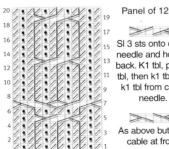

Panel of 12 sts

Sl 3 sts onto cable needle and hold at back. K1 tbl, p1, k1 tbl, then k1 tbl, p1, k1 tbl from cable needle.

As above but hold cable at front.

Panel of 10 sts

All k sts of cables are worked tbl.

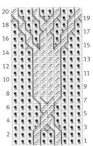

# Easy Cable Stitches

These cable stitches are relatively simple to learn but make attractive and versatile patterns.

## Easy Stitch 1

Multiple of 10 sts plus 2.

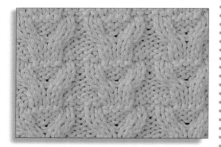

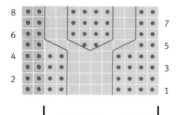

## Easy Stitch 2

Multiple of 12 sts.

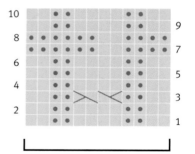

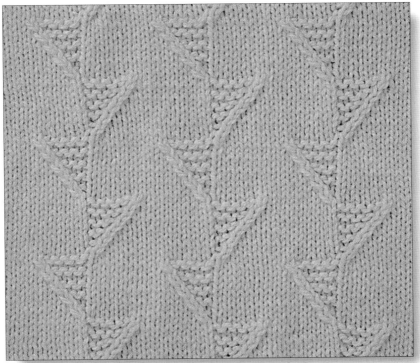

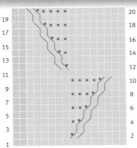

## Easy Stitch 3

Multiple of 14 sts plus 2.

## Easy Stitch 4

Panel of 16 sts.

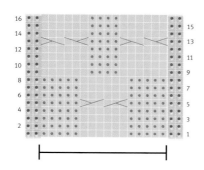

## Easy Stitch 5

Multiple of 10 sts plus 2.

Sl next 2 sts onto cable needle and hold at front, k2 then p2 from cable needle.

Sl next 2 sts onto cable needle, and hold at back, p2 then k2 from cable needle.

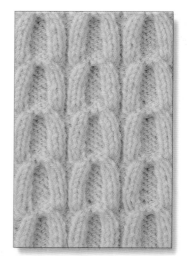

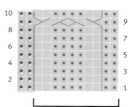

# Medium Cable Stitches

There are over 50 diverse cable stitches here for you to try. The patterns are diverse and attractive.

## Medium Stitch 1

Panel of 8 sts.

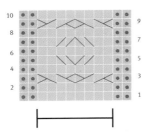

## Medium Stitch 2

Panel of 12 sts.

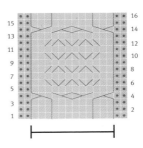

## Medium Stitch 3

Panel of 12 sts.

Sl 4 sts onto 1st cable needle, and hold at front, sl 4 sts on to 2nd cable needle and hold at back, k4, then k4 from 2nd cable needle, then k4 from 1st cable needle.

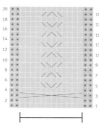

## Medium Stitch 4

Multiple of 15 sts plus 2.

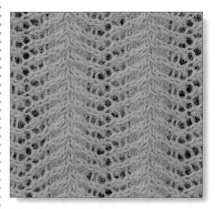

## Medium Stitch 5

Multiple of 12 sts plus 10.

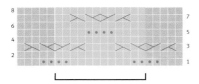

## Medium Stitch 6

Panel of 14 sts.

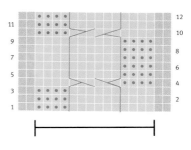

## Medium Stitch 7

Multiple of 17 sts plus 6.

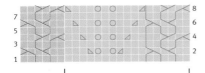

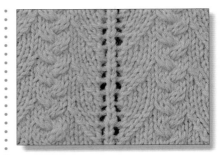

## Medium Stitch 8

Motif of 11 sts.

Sl 3 sts onto cable needle 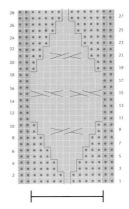 and hold at back, k2, then k3 from cable needle.

Sl 2 sts onto cable needle, and hold at front, k3 then k2 from cable needle.

## Medium Stitch 9

Panel of 12 sts.

Sl 3 sts onto cable needle and hold at back, p1, k1, p1, then k3 from cable needle.

Sl 3 sts onto cable needle and hold at front, k3 then k1, p1, k1 from cable needle.

Sl 3 sts onto cable needle and hold at back, k3 then p1, k1, p1 from cable needle.

Sl 3 sts onto cable needle and hold at front, k1, p1, k1, then k3 from cable needle.

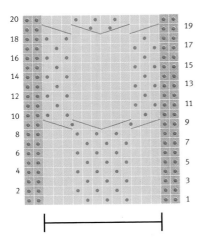

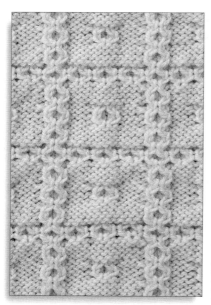

## Medium Stitch 10

Multiple of 16 sts plus 4.

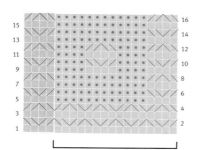

## Medium Stitch 11

Multiple of 23 sts plus 11.

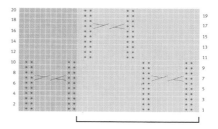

## Medium Stitch 12

Panel of 14 sts.

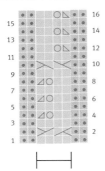

## Medium Stitch 13

Panel of 8 sts.

Sl 2 sts onto cable needle and hold at front, k4, then k2 from cable needle.

Sl 2 sts onto cable needle, and hold at front, k6, then k2 from cable needle.

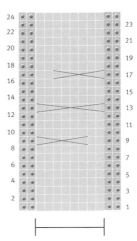

## Medium Stitch 14

Panel of 9 sts.

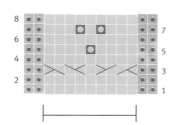

## Medium Stitch 15

Panel of 6 sts.

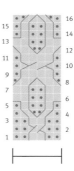

## Medium Stitch 16

Panel of 17 sts.

## Medium Stitch 17

Panel of 12 sts.

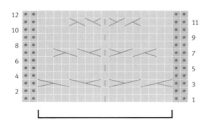

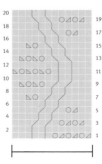

## Medium Stitch 18

Panel of 19 sts.

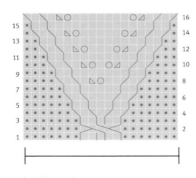

## Medium Stitch 19

Panel of 15 sts.

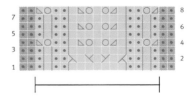

## Medium Stitch 20

Multiple of 11 sts.

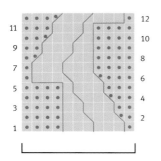

## Medium Stitch 21

Multiple of 12 sts plus 4.

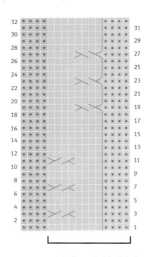

## Medium Stitch 22

Multiple of 12 sts plus 13.

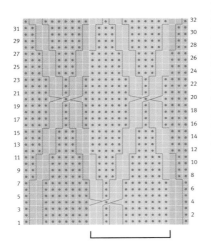

## Medium Stitch 23

Panel of 6 sts.

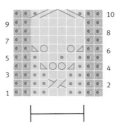

# Medium Stitch 24

Panel of 10 sts.

Sl 3 sts onto cable needle, and hold at back, k2 then p2, k1 from cable needle.

Sl 2 sts onto cable needle, and hold at front, k1, p2, then k2 from cable needle.

Sl 2 sts onto cable needle, and hold at front, k3, then k2 from cable needle.

Sl 3 sts onto cable needle, and hold at back, k2, then k3 from cable needle.

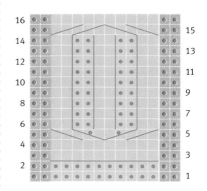

## Medium Stitch 25

Multiple of 20 sts plus 21.

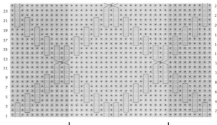

## Medium Stitch 26

Multiple of 8 sts plus 2.

Sl 3 sts onto cable needle,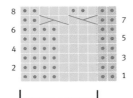
and hold at front, k1, p2, then k3 from
cable needle.

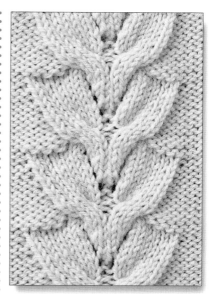

## Medium Stitch 27

Panel of 14 sts.

Sl next 3 sts onto cable needle and hold at back, p1, k2, then p3 from cable needle.

Sl next 3 sts onto cable needle and hold at front, p3, then k2, p1 from cable needle.

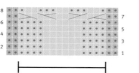

## Medium Stitch 28

Panel of 21 sts.

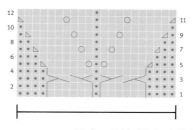

## Medium Stitch 29

Panel of 18 sts.

Sl 3 sts onto cable needle  and hold at front, k2, then k3 from cable needle.

Sl 2 sts onto cable needle and hold at back, k3, then k2 from cable needle.

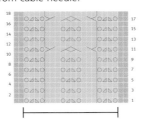

## Medium Stitch 30

Multiple of 18 sts.

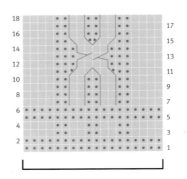

## Medium Stitch 31

Panel of 8 sts.

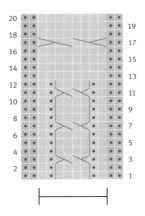

## Medium Stitch 32

Panel of 11 sts.

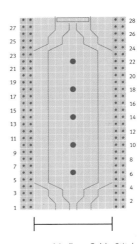

## Medium Stitch 33

Multiple of 6 sts plus 1.

Sl 1 st onto cable needle and hold at front, sl next 3 sts onto 2nd cable needle and hold at back, k1, then p3 from 2nd cable needle, then k1 from 1st cable needle.

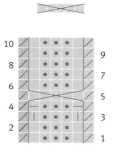

## Medium Stitch 34

Panel of 12 sts.

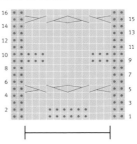

## Medium Stitch 35

Panel of 16 sts.

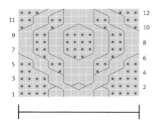

## Medium Stitch 36

Panel of
23 sts.

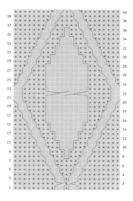

## Medium Stitch 37

Panel of 15 sts.

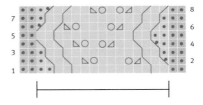

## Medium Stitch 38

Motif of 12 sts.

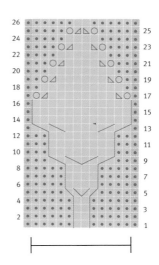

## Medium Stitch 39

Panel of 22 sts.

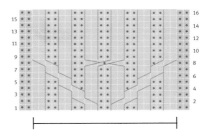

## Medium Stitch 40

Panel of 7 sts.

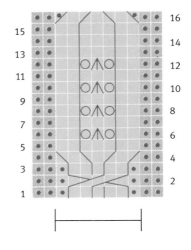

## Medium Stitch 41

Panel of 10 sts.

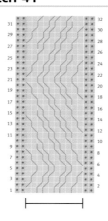

## Medium Stitch 42

Panel of 23 sts.

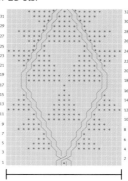

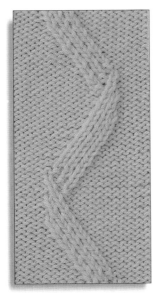

## Medium Stitch 43

Panel of 11 sts.

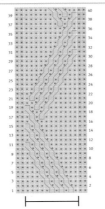

## Medium Stitch 44

Multiple of 12 sts.

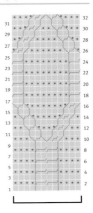

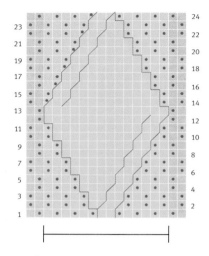

## Medium Stitch 45

Panel of 14 sts.

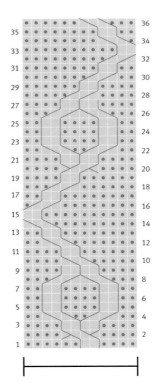

36
35
34
33
32
31
30
29
28
27
26
25
24
23
22
21
20
19
18
17
16
15
14
13
12
11
10
9
8
7
6
5
4
3
2
1

## Medium Stitch 46

Panel of 12 sts.

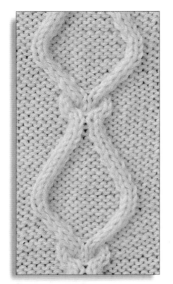

## Medium Stitch 47

Panel of 16 sts.

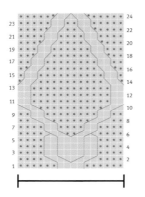

## Medium Stitch 48

Panel of 20 sts.

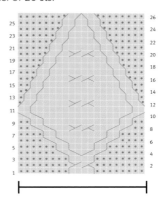

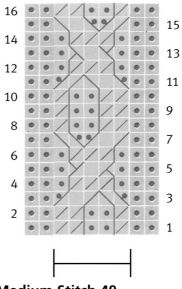

## Medium Stitch 49

Panel of 5 sts. All k sts of cables are worked tbl.

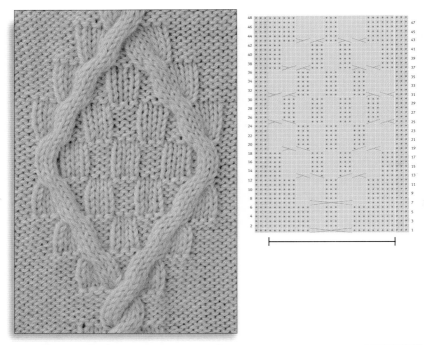

## Medium Stitch 50

Panel of 27 sts.

Sl next 3 sts onto cable needle and hold at back, k3, then p3 from cable needle.

Sl next 3 sts onto cable needle and hold at front, p3, then k3 from cable needle.

Sl next 6 sts onto cable needle and hold at back, k3, sl last 3 sts from cable needle to left-hand needle, p3, then k3 remaining sts from cable needle.

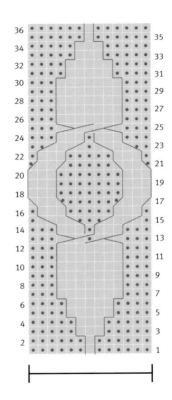

| | | | | | | | | | | | | | | | |
|36| | | | | | | | | | | | | | |35|

## Medium Stitch 51

Motif of 13 sts.

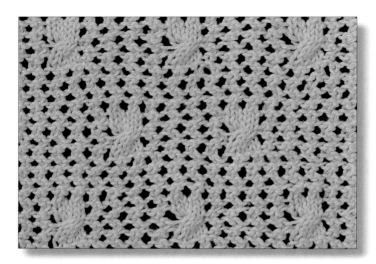

## Medium Stitch 52

Multiple of 12 sts plus 14.

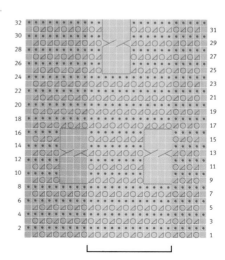

## Medium Stitch 53

Panel of 17 sts.

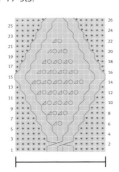

## Medium Stitch 54

Panel of 19 sts.

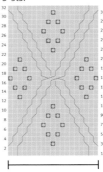

# Difficult Cable Stitches

There are over 40 cable stitches in this section. Many of them are complex to master, but the effects that you can achieve make the effort worthwhile.

## Difficult Stitch 1

Panel of 14 sts.

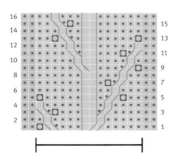

## Difficult Stitch 2

Multiple of 18 sts plus 10.

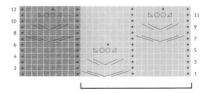

Sl 3 sts onto cable needle and hold at back, k1, and then k3 from cable needle, sl 1 st onto cable needle and hold at front, k3, then k1 from cable needle.

## Difficult Stitch 3

Panel of 9 sts.

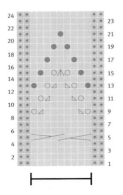

## Difficult Stitch 4

Panel of 12 sts.

Sl 2 sts onto cable needle, and hold at front, sl next 4 sts onto 2nd cable needle and hold at back, k2, then k4 from 2nd cable needle, then k2 from 1st cable needle.

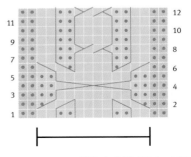

## Difficult Stitch 5

Motif of 9 sts.

Sl next 6 sts onto cable 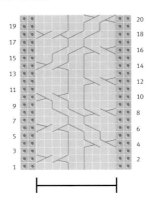 needles and hold at back, k1, p1, k1, then work 6 sts from cable needle: (p1, k1) 3 times

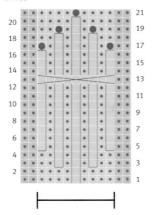

## Difficult Stitch 6

Panel of 10 sts.

# Difficult Stitch 7

Panel of 10 sts.

Sl next 2 sts onto cable needle and hold at front, p2, k2, then k2 from cable needle.

Sl next 4 sts onto cable needle, and hold at back, k2 then p4 from cable needle.

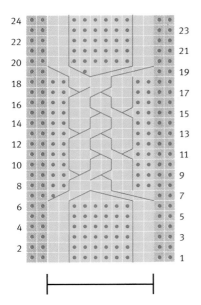

## Difficult Stitch 8

Panel of 30 sts.

## Difficult Stitch 9

Panel of 35 sts.

Sl next 5 sts onto cable needle and hold at back, p5, then work k2, p1, k2 from cable needle.

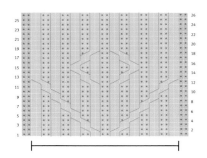

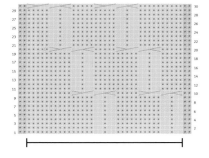

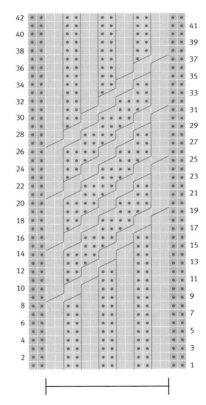

## Difficult Stitch 10

Panel of 14 sts.

## Difficult Stitch 11

Multiple of 24 sts plus 12.

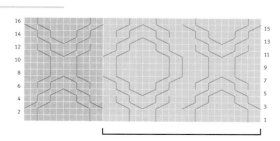

# Difficult Stitch 12

Panel of 43 sts.

# Difficult Stitch 13

Panel of 40 sts.

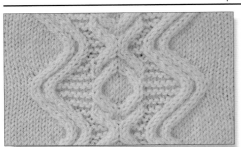

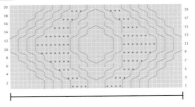

# Difficult Stitch 14

Panel of 9 sts.

Skpo, k1, K2 tog to make 3 sts from 5.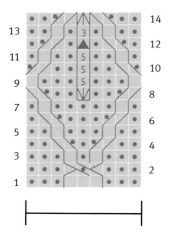

P5 on WS rows, k5 on RS rows.

(K1, yo, k1, yo, k1) in st to make 5 sts from 1.

P3.

## Difficult Stitch 15

Multiple of 26 sts plus 1.

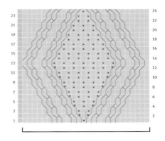

## Difficult Stitch 16

Panel of 8 sts.

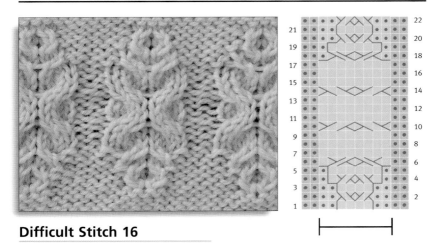

## Difficult Stitch 17

Motif of 19 sts.

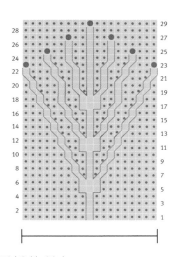

## Difficult Stitch 18

Motif of 19 sts.

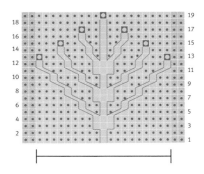

## Difficult Stitch 19

Panel of 19 sts.

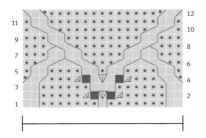

## Difficult Stitch 20

Panel of 10 sts.

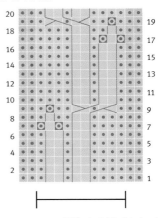

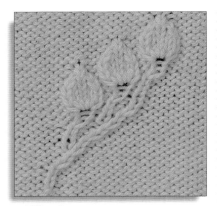

## Difficult Stitch 22

Panel of 11 sts.

## Difficult Stitch 21

Motif of
13 sts.

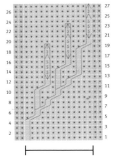

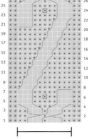

(K1, yo, k1, yo, ⓦ
k1) to make 5 sts
from 1.

P5 on WS rows, ⑤
k5 on RS rows.

Skpo, k1, k2tog ⚠
to make 3 sts
from 5.

P3. ③

Sl 2 sts ⟋⟋
onto cable
needle and hold at
back, k1, then p1,
k1 from cable
needle.

# Difficult Stitch 23

Panel of 24 sts.

Sl 4 sts onto cable needle and hold at back, k2, then k4 from cable needle.

Sl 2 sts onto cable needle and hold at front, k4, then k2 from cable needle.

Sl 4 sts onto cable needle and hold at back, k2, then work k4, p2 from cable needle.

Sl 2 sts onto cable needle and hold at front, p2, k2, then k2 from cable needle.

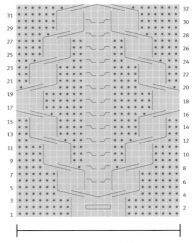

## Difficult Stitch 24

Panel of 20 sts.

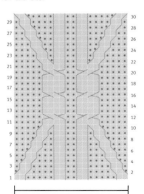

## Difficult Stitch 25

Mutiple of 16 sts plus 4.

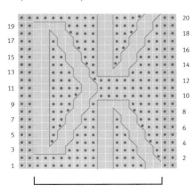

## Difficult Stitch 26

Mutiple of 10 sts plus 10.

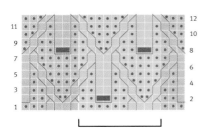

## Difficult Stitch 27

Panel of 5 sts.
All k sts of
cables are
worked tbl.

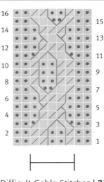

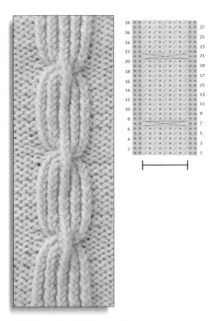

## Difficult Stitch 28

Panel of 9 sts.

Sl 3 sts onto 1st cable
needle, and hold at back,
sl next 3 sts onto 2nd cable needle and
hold at front, k1 tbl, p1, k1 tbl. Then
work sts from 2nd cable needle p1, k1
tbl, pl, then work sts from 1st cable
needle k1 tbl, p1, k1 tbl.

## Difficult Stitch 29

Panel of 25 sts.

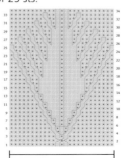

## Difficult Stitch 30

## Difficult Stitch 31

Panel of 15 sts. All k sts of cables are worked tbl.

Panel of 19 sts. All k sts of cables are worked tbl.

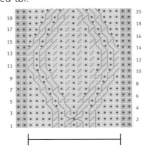

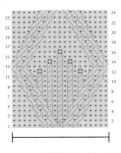

# Difficult Stitch 32

Panel of 15 sts.

Sl 1 st onto cable needle and hold at back, k1 tbl (p1, k1 tbl) twice, then p1 from cable needle.

Sl 5 sts onto cable needle and hold at front, p1, then work k1 tbl (p1, k1 tbl) twice from cable needle.

Sl 6 sts onto cable needle and hold at back, k1 tbl (p1, k1 tbl) twice, then work sts from cable needle (p1, k1 tbl) 3 times.

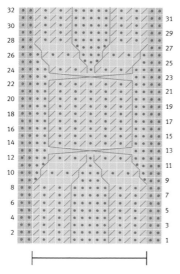

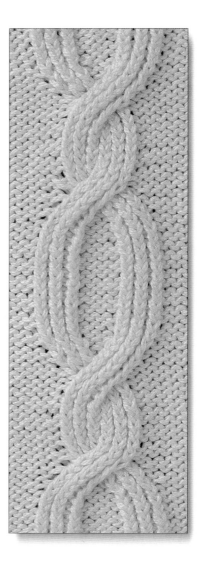

# Difficult Stitch 33

Panel of 16 sts.

Sl 2 sts onto cable needle and hold at back, k2, then p1, k1 tbl from cable needle.

Sl 2 sts onto cable needle and hold at front, k1 tbl, p1, then k2 sts from cable needle.

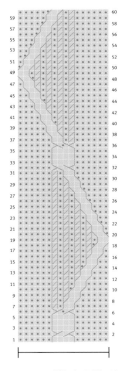

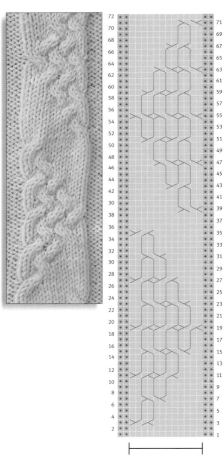

## Difficult Stitch 35

Panel of 17 sts.

Sl 3 sts onto
cable needle
and hold at
back, k4, then
k3 from cable
needle.

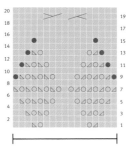

## Difficult Stitch 34

Panel of 12 sts.

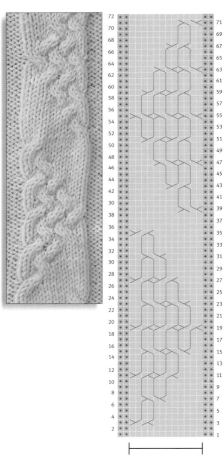

228 | Cable Stitches

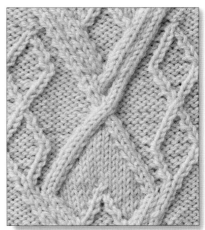

## Difficult Stitch 36

Multiple of 12 sts plus 14.

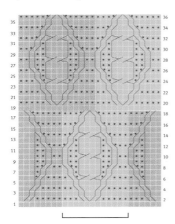

## Difficult Stitch 37

Panel of 32 sts.

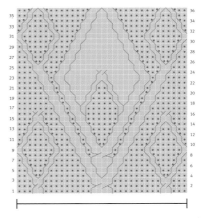

## Difficult Stitch 38

Motif of 27 sts.

## Difficult Stitch 39

Motif of 22 sts.

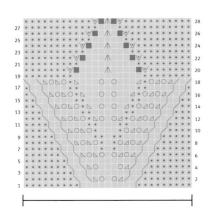

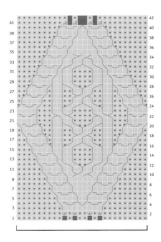

## Difficult Stitch 40

Panel of 31 sts.

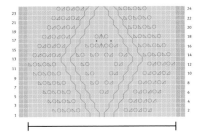

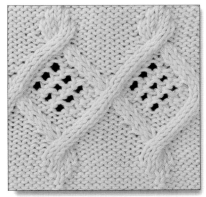

## Difficult Stitch 41

Multiple of 13 sts plus 13.

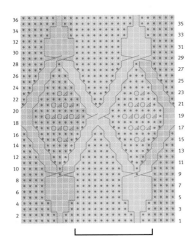

## Difficult Stitch 42

Panel of 17 sts.

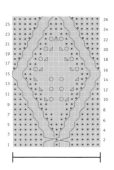

## Difficult Stitch 43

Multiple of 14 sts plus 15.

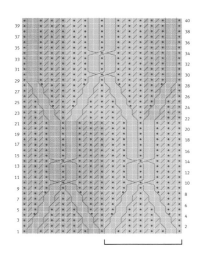

## Difficult Stitch 44

Panel of 50 sts.

## Difficult Stitch 45

Panel of 41 sts.

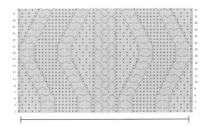

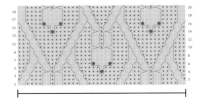

# Lace and Bobble Stitches

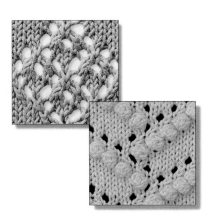

# Popular Lace Stitches

The easiest lace patterns have each increase worked next to the corresponding decrease, so the stitch count stays the same on every row. In other patterns, the increases and decreases occur at different places along the row, but you'll find these just as easy to work, as the total number of stitches on each row doesn't change. For some beautiful laces, the increases and decreases are made on different rows, making it harder to keep track of the stitch count, but creating exquisite patterns. Adding a border or edging can transform a plain piece of knitting.

Your choice of yarn will affect the appearance of your lace knitting. Firm, smooth yarns will make the construction more visible; soft or brushed yarns will blur the pattern. Traditionally, very fine wool or cotton is worked on relatively large needles. When the work is pressed, the delicate texture of the lace is revealed. Lace edgings tend to work better in a crisp, fine yarn such as cotton, since this gives clear stitch definition, and is less likely to stretch. Avoid leaving the piece halfway through a pattern repeat, as lace can be quite difficult to unpick.

## Making Yarn-Overs

It's essential to take the yarn over the needle so that the strand lies in the same direction as the other stitches. Working into this strand on the next row makes a hole, but if the strand is twisted, the hole will close up. When the stitch before a yarn-over is purl, the yarn will already be at the front, ready to go over the needle.

Some lace patterns have larger holes made by working two or more yarn-overs together. The extra yarn-overs may be dropped on the following row, so that only one stitch is increased, or they may all be worked so that several stitches are made.

For making both single and multiple yarn-overs, see pages 55–56.

## Creating Lace Patterns

Using the same decreases with yarn-over increases, but placing them next to each other or spacing them apart creates quite different effects.

In example A, the zigzag has the decreases separated from the yarn-overs, so that they form gently wandering lines up the fabric. In example B, working increases and decreases only on right-side rows creates a steep angled chevron. In example C, the decreases are worked immediately to one side of the yarn-overs, outlining the zigzags. In example D, the patterning is on every row, giving a lacier appearance as well as a less sharply angled chevron.

Example B

Example C

Example A

Example D

## Feather and Fan

This is an old Shetland lace stitch with many variations. Common to them all is the grouping of increases and decreases separately along the row to make patterns resembling feathers, fans, waves and scallops.

## Old Shale

This version of a famous Shetland lace stitch is particularly simple and rhythmic.

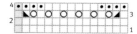

Multiple of 12 sts plus 1.

◢   Multiple of 12 sts plus 1.

◢   Multiple of 12 sts plus 1.

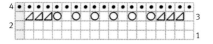

Multiple of 18 sts plus 1.

## Small Hearts

These two simple hearts could be used as repeat patterns or scattered among other motifs.

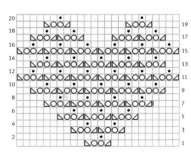

Motif of 13 sts.

Motif of 11 sts.

△ K2 TOG, RETURN ST TO LEFT NEEDLE, PASS NEXT ST OVER IT, SL ST BACK ON TO RIGHT NEEDLE

## Picot Heart

The double eyelets that make this heart have themselves a heart shape, made by working p1, k1 into the double yarn-over, instead of the usual k1, p1.

Motif of 24 sts.

## Pierced Heart

Yarn-over increases and their corresponding decreases help to shape this heart as well as decorate it.

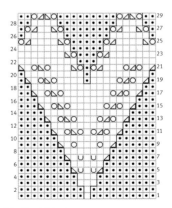

Motif of 21 sts.

## Scotch Faggot Cable

Cabling a faggot rib creates a stitch that can be used as an all-over repeat or in conjunction with other open stitches.

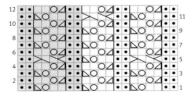

Multiple of 12 sts plus 8.

## Lace Ladder

Very smooth and controlled, this ladder is quite stable in spite of its open texture.

Multiple of 4 sts plus 2.

## Bird's Eye

All-over double eyelets make an unusally textured pattern.

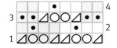

Multiple of 4 sts plus 4.

## Candlelight

Lace knitting lends itself to flame- and leaf-like patterns. In each of these motifs, the decreases move away from the increases, pulling the stiches into outlines.

## Diamond Spiral

This simple but sophisticated panel would work well alongside cables.

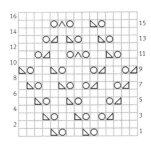

Panel of 15 sts.

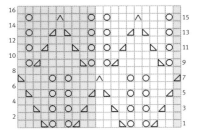

Panel of 10 sts plus 11.

## Falling Leaves

This pattern is similar to Candlelight in construction, but the decreases pull the stitches in to form the central vein of each leaf.

## Paired Leaves

The increases and decreases form drooping leaves with veins, and make the lower edge strongly shaped.

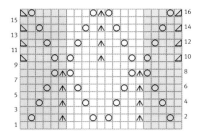

Multiple of 10 sts plus 11.

Panel of 29 sts.

## Feather Lace

Here, increases outline long, feather-like shapes.

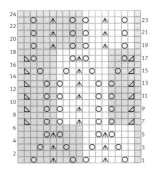

Multiple of 8 sts plus 3.

## Gothic Lace

This is a progression of Feather Lace. One repeat of the chart makes a border, while repeating rows 1 to 16 produces an all-over pattern.

Multiple of 8 sts plus 1.

# Popular Bobble Stitches

A group of increased stitches, decreased abruptly, makes a knot, or a bobble, which can be used to add emphasis to a familiar cable or lace pattern.

Knots are worked into one stitch and completed without turning the work. Bobbles are also worked into one stitch, but have extra rows added by turning and working the bobble stitches only. Bobbles, knots and leaves are often worked on a reverse stockinette background to emphasize the contrast.

Larger groups of decorative increases and decreases worked over several rows make a blister – a flat, raised shape – or a leaf. There is also a family of all-over textured popcorn and blackberry stitches, made from repeated groups of increases and decreases that alternate on following rows. To make easy three- and five-stitch bobbles, see page 61.

## Making a Seven-Stitch Leaf

These three same-size leaves are each made slightly differently. But in all of them, pairs of increases are followed by pairs of decreases, worked at the sides or in the center.

**Leaf 1**
This leaf has yarn-overs each side of the center stitch.

**Leaf 2**
Invisible lifted strand increases the shape of the base of the leaf.

**Leaf 3**
Seven stitches are worked into a double yarn-over at the start of this leaf.

## Blackberry Stitch

This all-over nubby pattern is also known as "trinity stitch," because three stitches are made from one, and one from three on alternate rows.

Multiple of 4 sts.

Ⅴ  [K1, p1, k1] all in one st.

⚠  P3 tog.

## Knotted Rib

Here, the very smallest possible knot adds texture to the smooth surface of a rib stitch worked through the back of the loop.

⊙  K into front, back and front of st making 3 sts from 1, lift 2nd and 1st sts over 3rd and off needle.

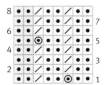

Multiple of 6 sts plus 2.

## Two and Three Bobble Rib

Crunchy bobbles are worked so closely together in this pattern that they make the rib spread out instead of pulling in.

⑤ [K1, yo, k1, yo, k1] all into 1 st making 5 sts from one, turn k5, turn p5, lift 4th, 3rd, 2nd and 1st sts over 5th and off needle.

Multiple of 5 sts plus 2.

## Bobble Blocks

Purl-stitch bobbles are placed in regular rows on stockinette stitch blocks, and outlined in alternating knit and purl stitches.

⑤ [K1, yo, k1, yo, k1] all into 1 st, turn k5, turn, skpo, k3 tog, lift 1st st over 2nd and off needle.

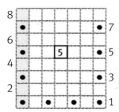

## Bobble and Wave

The wave rib is not cabled – it's made with increases and decreases. The bobbles add an accent at the curve of each wave. For ⓢ , see Two and Three Bobble Rib, page 247.

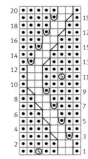

Multiple of 8 sts.

## Bobble and Braid Cable

This cable panel uses five-stitch cross, so there is a center stitch to place the bobble on. For ⓢ , see Two and Three Bobble Rib, page 247.

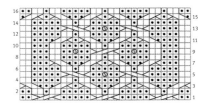

Panel of 29 sts.

## Triple Nosegay

The traditional nosegay pattern has just two branches with four bobbles. Here the stitch pattern has been extended to three branches and six bobbles. For 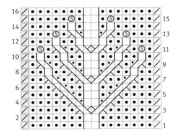, see Two and Three Bobble Rib, page 247.

Panel of 17 sts plus 1.

## Three Bobble Cable

Cabled ovals enclose three crunchy purl-stitch bobbles. Again, the large cable cross uses five stitches to give a center stitch to place the bobble on. For ⑤, see Two and Three Bobble Rib, page 247.

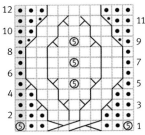

Multiple of 10 sts plus 1.

# Easy Lace Stitches

These lace stitches are relatively easy to learn how to knit.

## Easy Stitch 1

Multiple of 6 sts plus 4.

## Easy Stitch 2

Multiple of 5 sts plus 3.

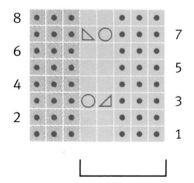

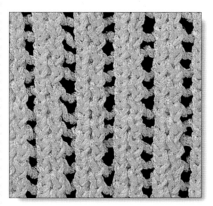

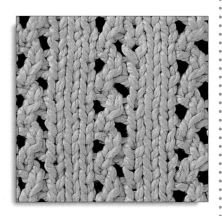

## Easy Stitch 3

Multiple of 5 sts plus 3.

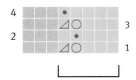

## Easy Stitch 4

Multiple of 4 sts plus 2.

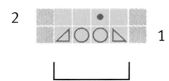

## Easy Stitch 5

Multiple of 10 sts plus 6.

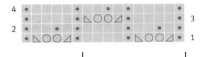

## Easy Stitch 6

Multiple of 10 sts plus 5.

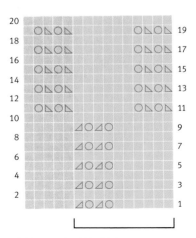

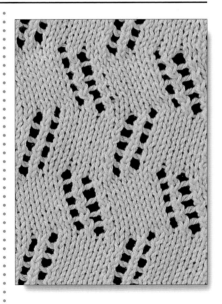

# Medium Lace and Bobble Stitches

These stitches can be used to add interesting effects to your creations.

## Medium Stitch 1

The berry motifs are arranged as a half-drop pattern here. you could also try repeating just the first 12 rows.

⊘ [K1, yo, k1] all into 1 st making 3 sts from one, turn k3, turn p3, lift 2nd an 1st sts over 3rd and off needle.

Multiple of 12 sts plus 1.

## Medium Stitch 2

These pretty little motifs have slender leaves, because the open increases are taken into the reverse stockinette stitch background. For ⊘ , see page 247.

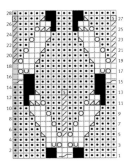

Multiple of 14 sts plus 1.

## Medium Stitch 3

Regular increases and decreases give a slightly raised surface to this pattern. Despite making and losing stitches on each right-side row, this is not difficult to work because the stitch count remains constant.

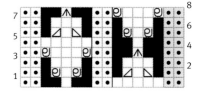 Lift strand between st but do not twist strand when knitting into it to make a small hole.

Multiple of 14 sts plus 1.

## Medium Stitch 4

To work a frilled edging, cast on a multiple of 12 sts plus 4, then start with 3rd row, k8 where cast-on stitches are indicated. Follow the chart and you'll end with a stitch count that's a multiple of four.

Cast on 1 st by the loop method, twisting the loop before placing it on the needle.

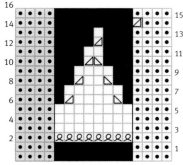

Multiple of 4 sts plus 4.

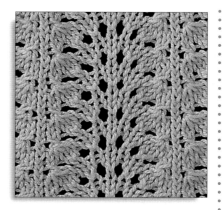

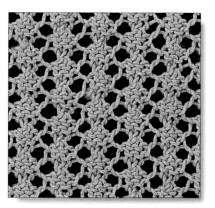

## Medium Stitch 5

Multiple of 14 sts plus 1.

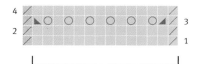

## Medium Stitch 6

Multiple of 6 sts plus 5.

K4 tog

K4 tog tbl

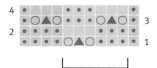

## Medium Stitch 7

Multiple of 10 sts plus 7.

(K1, yo, k1,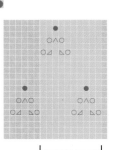
yo, k1) in
st to make
5 sts from
1, turn, p5,
turn, k3,
k2tog, pass
3 sts, one
at a time,
over k2tog.

## Medium Stitch 8

Panel of 23 sts.

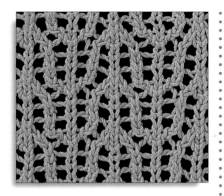

## Medium Stitch 9

Multiple of 8 sts plus 1.

## Medium Stitch 10

Multiple of 10 sts plus 1.

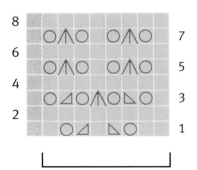

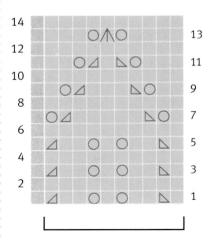

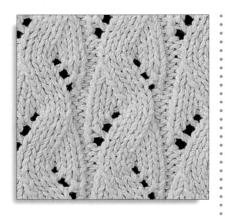

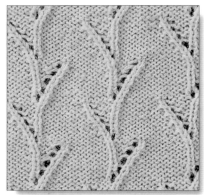

## Medium Stitch 11

Multiple of 8 sts plus 2.

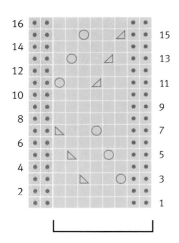

## Medium Stitch 12

Multiple of 13 sts plus 2.

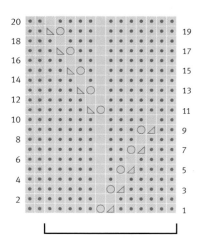

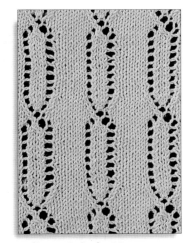

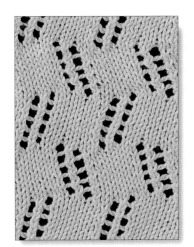

## Medium Stitch 13

Multiple of 11 sts.

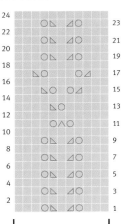

## Medium Stitch 14

Multiple of 10 sts plus 5.

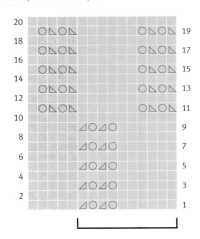

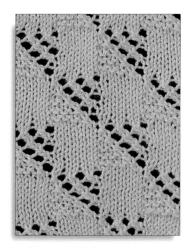

## Medium Stitch 15

Multiple of 12 sts plus 2.

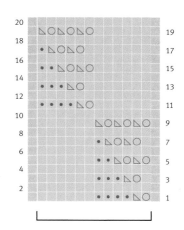

## Medium Stitch 16

Panel of 9 sts.

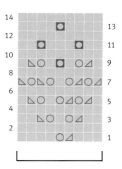

## Medium Stitch 17

Panel of 13 sts.

(K1, p1, k1, p1, k1) in st to make 5 sts from 1, turn, k5, turn, pass 2nd, 3rd, 4th and 5th sts over 1st, k in back of this st.

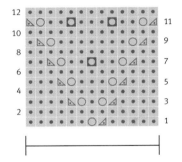

## Medium Stitch 18

Multiple of 11 sts plus 1.

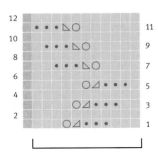

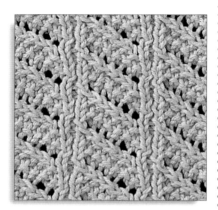

## Medium Stitch 19

Multiple of 9 sts plus 1.

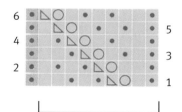

## Medium Stitch 20

Panel of 17 sts.

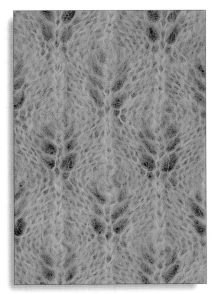

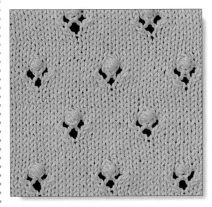

## Medium Stitch 21

Multiple of 10 sts plus 11.

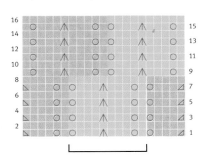

## Medium Stitch 22

Multiple of 10 sts plus 7.

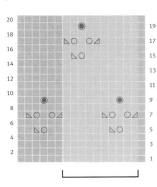

## Medium Stitch 23

Multiple of 12 sts plus 7.

## Medium Stitch 24

Multiple of 10 sts plus 1.

K2tog through back of loops.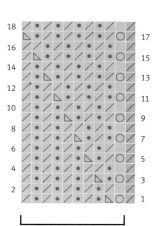

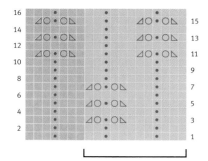

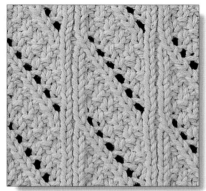

## Medium Stitch 25

Motif of 17 sts.

## Medium Stitch 26

Multiple of 9 sts plus 1.

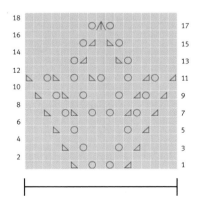

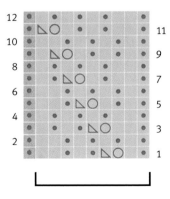

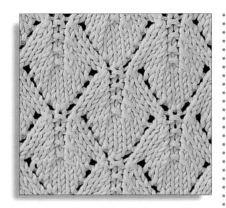

## Medium Stitch 27

Multiple of 12 sts plus 1.

## Medium Stitch 28

Multiple of 11 sts plus 2.

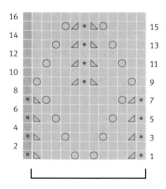

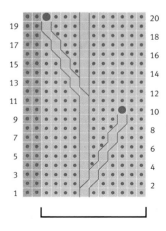

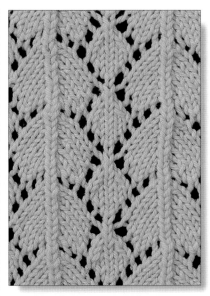

## Medium Stitch 29

Panel of 14 sts.

## Medium Stitch 30

Multiple of 12 sts plus 13.

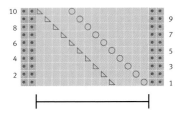

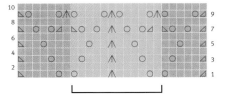

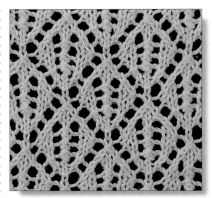

## Medium Stitch 31

Multiple of 16 sts plus 1.

## Medium Stitch 32

Multiple of 10 sts plus 13.

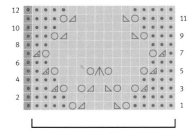

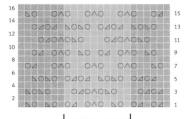

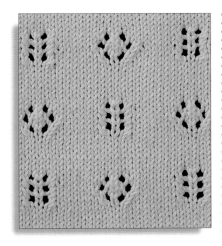

## Medium Stitch 33

Multiple of 22 sts plus 13.

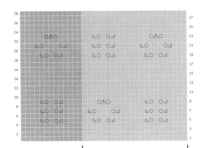

## Medium Stitch 34

Multiple of 10 sts plus 3.

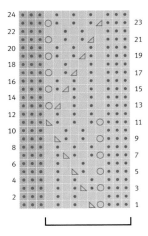

## Medium Stitch 35

Multiple of 12 sts plus 3.

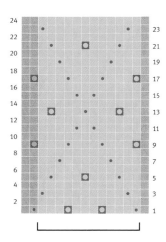

## Medium Stitch 36

Multiple of 22 sts plus 1.

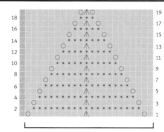

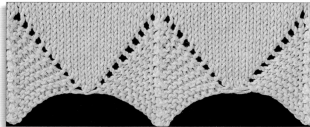

## Medium Stitch 37

Multiple of 16 sts plus 17.

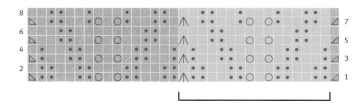

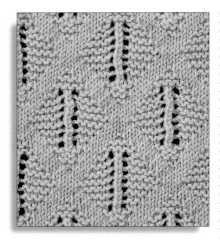

## Medium Stitch 39

Motif of 16 sts.

## Medium Stitch 38

Multiple of 16 sts plus 17.

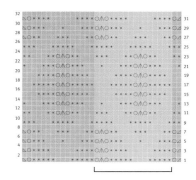

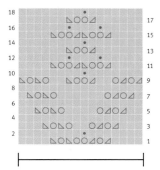

## Medium Stitch 40

Motif of 15 sts.

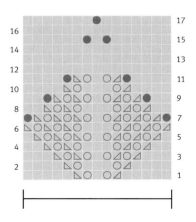

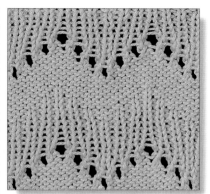

## Medium Stitch 41

Multiple of 12 sts plus 3.

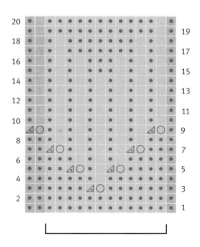

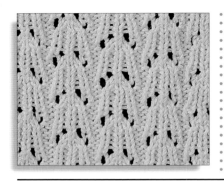

## Medium Stitch 42

Multiple of 14 sts plus 9.

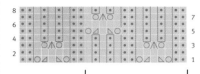

## Medium Stitch 43

Panel of 16 sts.

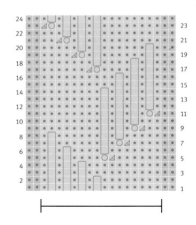

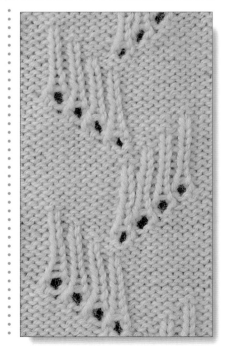

## Medium Stitch 44

Panel of 18 sts.

Sl next 3 sts onto right-hand needle, k in front and back of next st, k2, pass 3 slipped sts over 4 sts just worked.

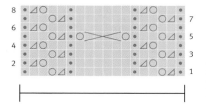

## Medium Stitch 45

Multiple of 9 sts plus 11.

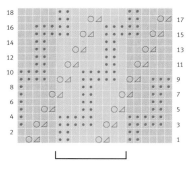

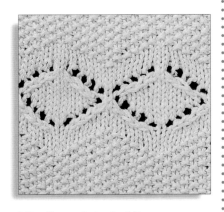

## Medium Stitch 46

Multiple of 12 sts plus 13.

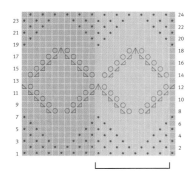

## Medium Stitch 47

Motif of 13 sts.

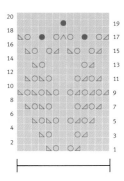

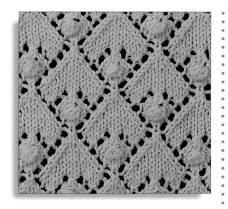

## Medium Stitch 48

Multiple of 12 sts plus 13.

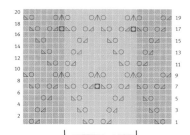

## Medium Stitch 49

Motif of 13 sts.

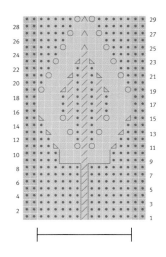

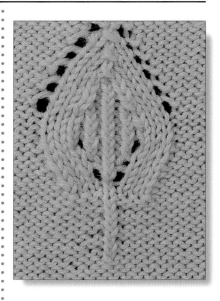

# Medium Stitch 50

Panel of 7 sts.

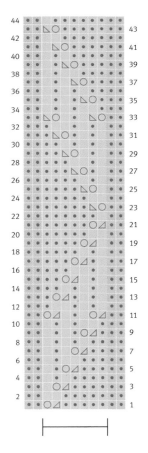

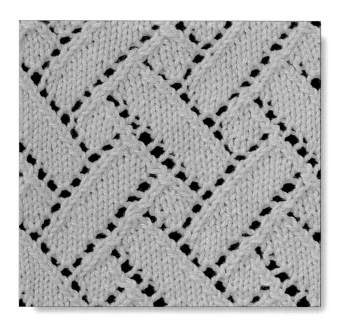

## Medium Stitch 51

Multiple of 12 sts plus 15.

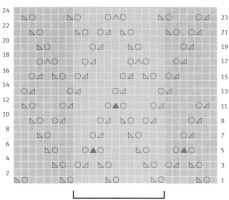

## Medium Stitch 52

Multiple of 16 sts plus 9.

(K1, p1, k1, p1, k1, p1, k1) in st to 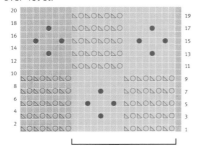 make 7 sts from 1, pass 2nd, 3rd, 4th, 5th, 6th and 7th sts, one at a time, over 1st st.

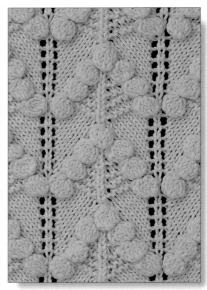

## Medium Stitch 53

Multiple of 18 sts plus 1.

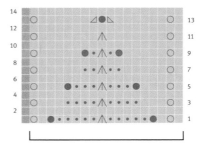

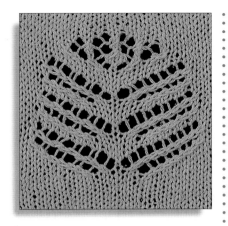

## Medium Stitch 54

Motif of 23 sts.

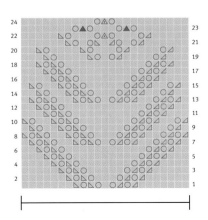

## Medium Stitch 55

Motif of 17 sts.

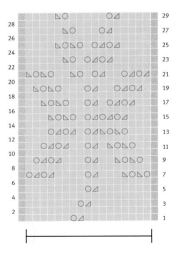

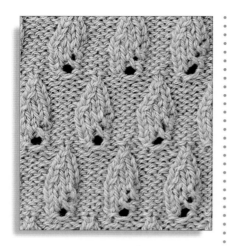

## Medium Stitch 56

Multiple of 6 sts plus 5.

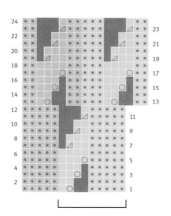

## Medium Stitch 57

Multiple of 12 sts plus 3.

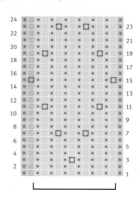

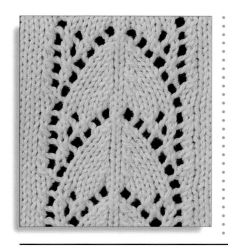

## Medium Stitch 58

Panel of 17 sts.

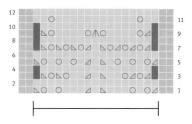

## Medium Stitch 59

Multiple of 12 sts plus 13.

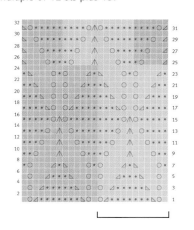

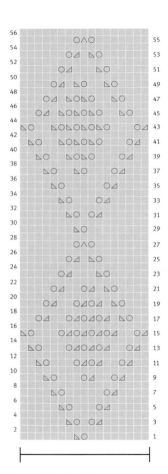

## Medium Stitch 60

Panel of 17 sts.

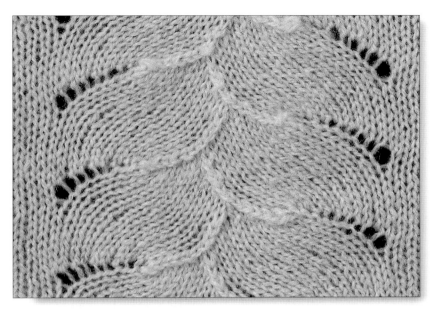

## Medium Stitch 61

Panel of 37 sts.

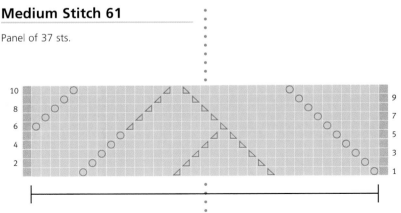

## Medium Stitch 62

Motif of 23 sts.

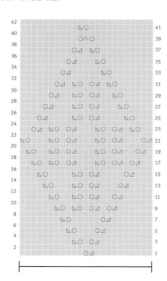

## Medium Stitch 63

Motif of 17 sts.

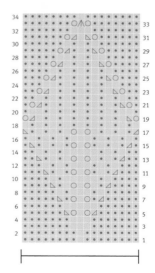

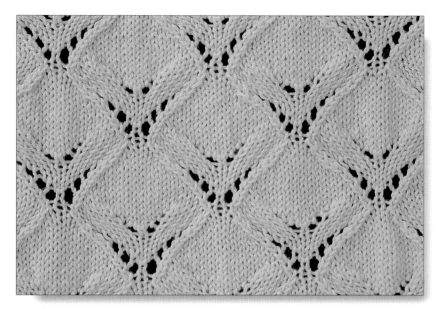

## Medium Stitch 64

Multiple of 20 sts
plus 21.

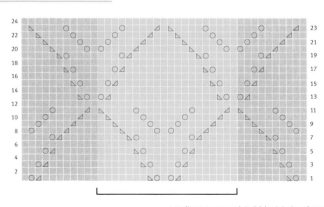

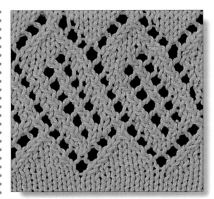

## Medium Stitch 65

Motif of 17 sts.

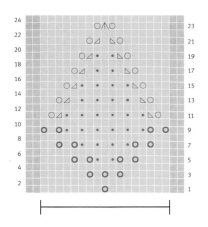

## Medium Stitch 66

Multiple of 8 sts plus 8.

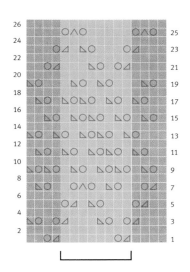

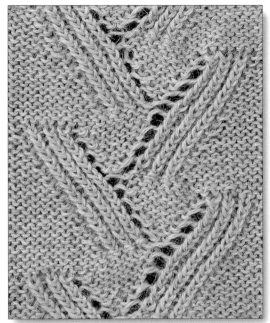

## Medium Stitch 67

Panel of 26 sts.

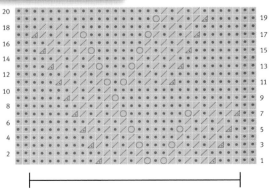

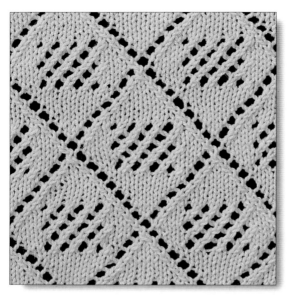

## Medium Stitch 68

Multiple of 16 sts plus 19.

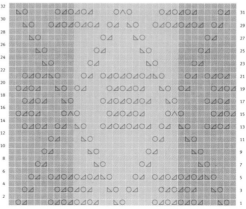

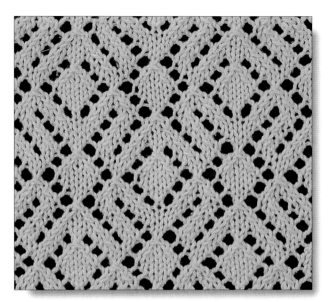

# Medium
# Stitch 69

Multiple of 16 sts
plus 19.

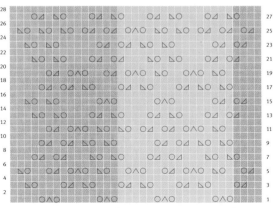

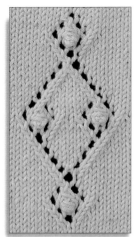

## Medium Stitch 70

Motif of
15 sts.

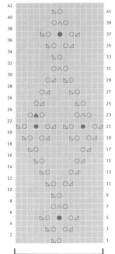

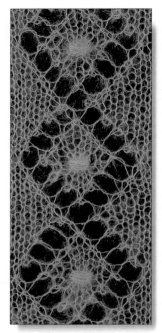

## Medium Stitch 71

Panel of
13 sts.

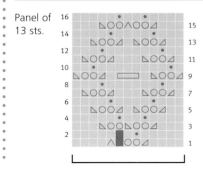

# Medium
## Stitch 72

Multiple of 18 sts plus 21.

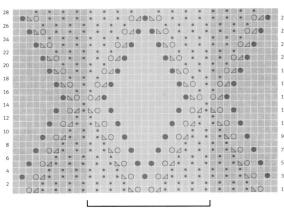

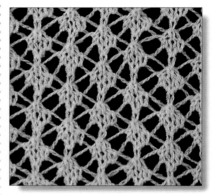

## Medium Stitch 73

Multiple of 13 sts plus 15.

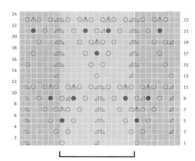

## Medium Stitch 74

Multiple of 6 sts plus 6.

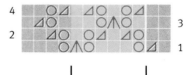

# Difficult Lace and Bobble Stitches

Three-dimensional bobbles complement
the round, open eyelets of lace stitches
perfectly.

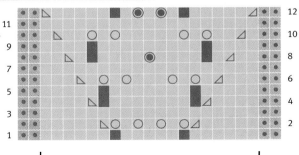

## Difficult Stitch 1

Panel of 17 sts.

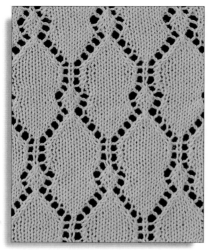

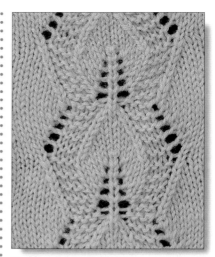

## Difficult Stitch 2

## Difficult Stitch 3

Multiple of 12 sts plus 13.

Panel of 19 sts.

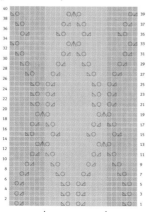

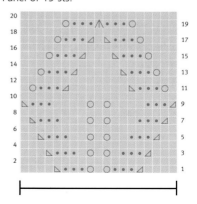

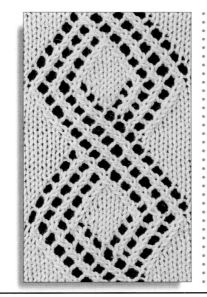

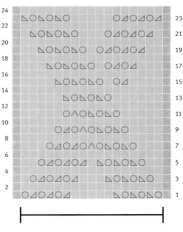

## Difficult Stitch 4

Panel of 17 sts.

## Difficult Stitch 5

Multiple of 12 sts plus 4.

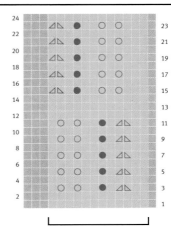

## Difficult Stitch 6

Multiple of 12 sts plus 3.

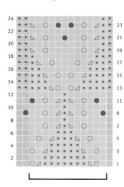

## Difficult Stitch 7

Panel of 23 sts.

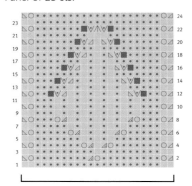

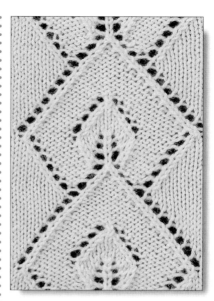

## Difficult Stitch 8

Motif of 15 sts.

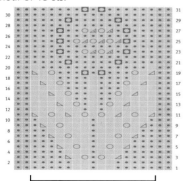

## Difficult Stitch 9

Panel of 23 sts.

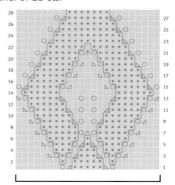

## Difficult Stitch 10

Multiple of 16 sts plus 18.

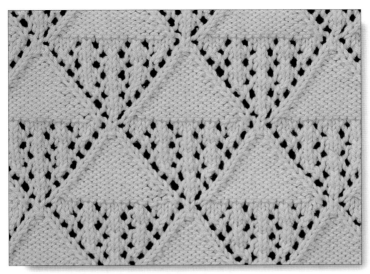

## Difficult Stitch 11

Multiple of 18 sts plus 19.

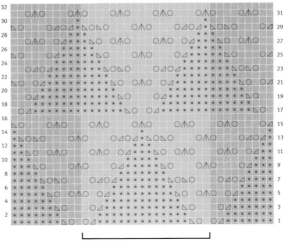

## Difficult Stitch 12

Panel of 2 sts.

Sl 1 st onto cable needle, and hold at front [k1, yo] twice in next st, then k1 st from cable needle.

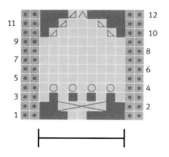

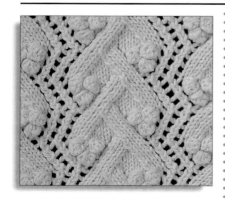

## Difficult Stitch 13

Multiple of 18 sts plus 5.

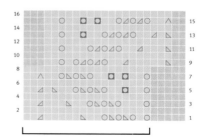

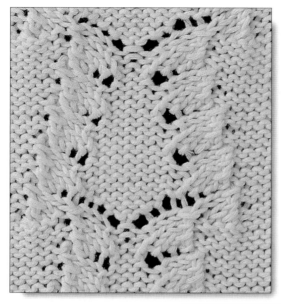

## Difficult Stitch 14

Panel of 19 sts.

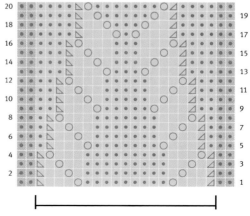

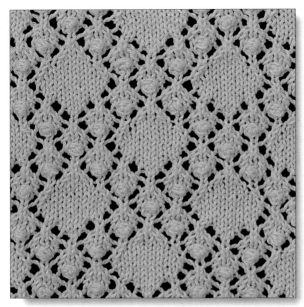

## Difficult Stitch 15

Multiple of 18 sts plus 13.

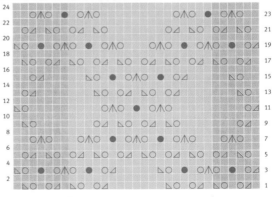

## Difficult Stitch 17

Motif of 13 sts.

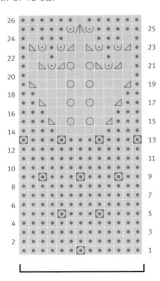

## Difficult Stitch 16

Motif of
8 sts.

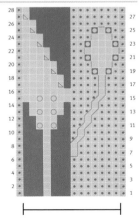

# Easy Lace Edging Stitches

These stitches offer some really attractive ways to complete a design.

## Fern Edging

This leafy edging in garter stitch has large eyelets made with multiple yarn-overs.

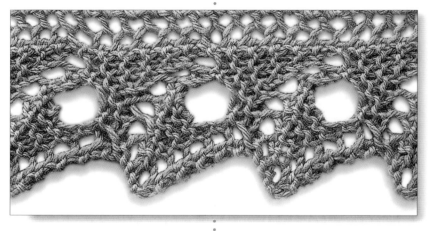

Cast on 10 stitches

K2 tog    ⊿

Cast off    − − −

St remaining after casting off    ✳

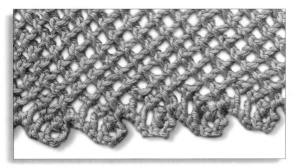

Cast on 14 stitches

Cast off     - - -

St remaining after    ✳
casting off

## Mesh Lace Edging

As the pattern is based on garter stitch,
either side can be used as the right side.
This picture shows the smooth side.

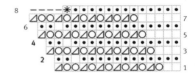

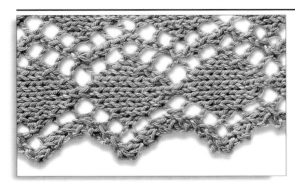

## Diamond Edging

This is a classic edging that has many
uses. It requires careful pressing to open
out the lace.

Cast on 10 stitches.
Repeat rows 3–14.

# Medium Lace Edging Stitches

Here are some more ideas for finishing
off your knitting creations.

## Medium Stitch 1

Cast on 6 sts.

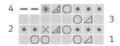

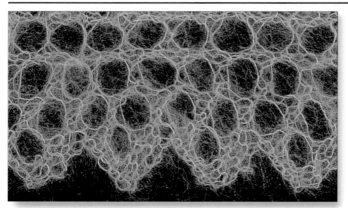

## Medium Stitch 2

Cast on 11 sts.

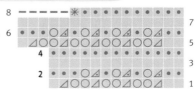

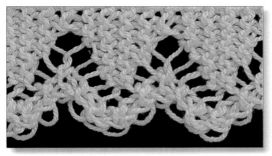

## Medium Stitch 3

Cast on 7 sts.

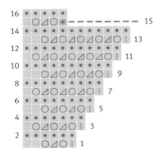

## Medium Stitch 4

Cast on 5 sts.

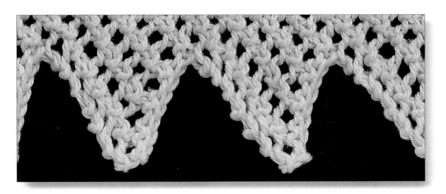

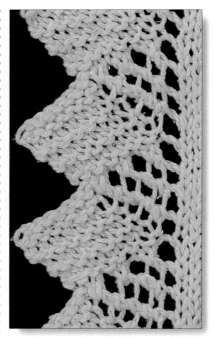

## Medium Stitch 5

Cast on 6 sts.

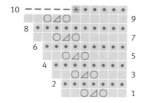

## Medium Stitch 6

Cast on 10 sts.

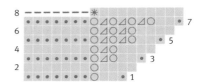

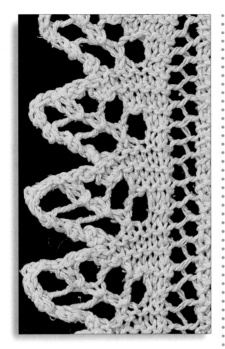

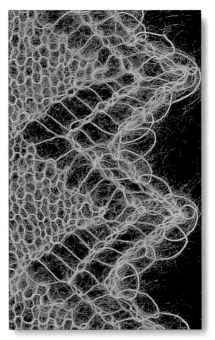

## Medium Stitch 7

Cast on 10 sts.

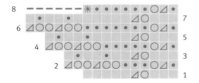

## Medium Stitch 8

Cast on 7 sts.

# Difficult Lace Edging Stitches

These intricate lace edging stitches will add stunning finishing touches to your knitting.

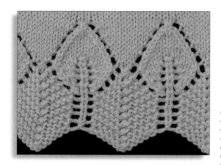

## Difficult Stitch 1

Multiple of 14 sts plus 15.

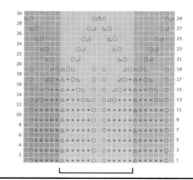

## Difficult Stitch 2

Cast on 19 sts.

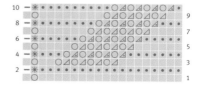

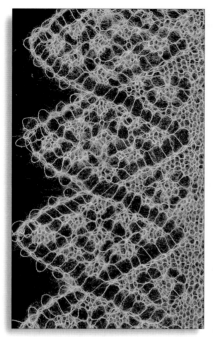

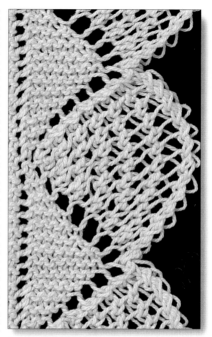

## Difficult Stitch 3

Cast on 15 sts.

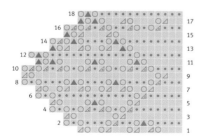

## Difficult Stitch 4

Cast on 12 sts.

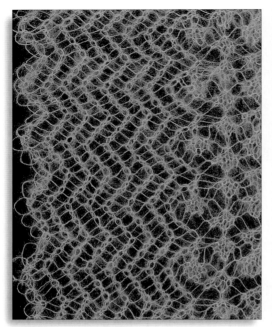

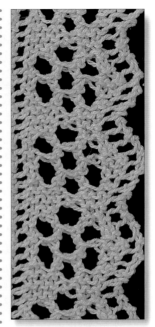

## Difficult Stitch 5

Cast on 32 sts.

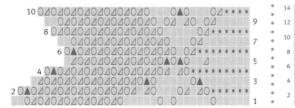

## Difficult Stitch 6

Cast on 12 sts.

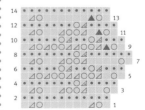

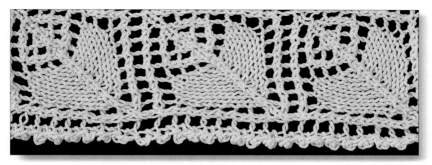

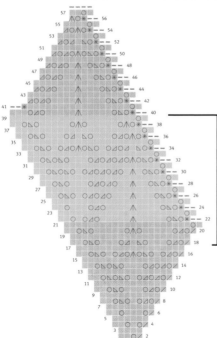

## Difficult Stitch 7

Cast on 3 sts.

Work rows 1–21,
then work rows
22–39 for
required length,
then work rows
40–57, and cast off remaining
4 sts.

# Twist Stitches

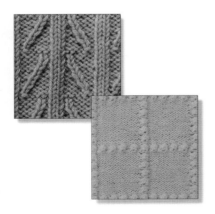

# Popular Twist Stitches

Twisting two stitches by working the second before the first gives a similar appearance to a one-over-one cable. Large areas can be worked where it would be tedious to cable. Twist stitches give a linear, raised texture to the surface and contract the fabric. To open it up, increases are worked below and decreases above the twist stitch areas, or eyelets are used.

Twists are sometimes combined with cable stitch patterns, with the shallower twists complementing the depths of the cables. The advantage of twist stitches is that they can be worked more quickly than cable stitches.

Although twists are easy to do, there are lots of tiny but important variations that change the appearance of a twist. They can be worked on right- or wrong-side rows, and the stitches can be all knit, all purl or a combination of the two. Twist stitch patterns are easy to work in the round from a chart, especially the patterns that move a stitch on every row. Simply read every row of the chart from right to left, interpreting all the symbols as right-side-row twists.

## • How to Work a Left Twist

This twist is worked on a right-side row. As the stitches change place, the first stitch lies on top and slants to the left, while the stitch behind is worked through the back of the loop.

To begin, knit into the back of the second stitch.

The second stage is to knit into the front of the first stage.

Finally, slip both stitches off the left needle together.

## • Left Twist Variations

To work a knit-and-purl two-stitch slanting to the left, purl into the back of the second stitch, then knit into the front of the first stitch. To twist two stitches to the left on a wrong-side row, purl into the back of the second stitch, then purl into the front of the first stitch.

## • How to Work a Right Twist

In this right-sided row twist, the second stitch lies on top and slants to the right, while the stitch behind is worked through the back of the loop.

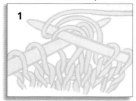

**1** To begin, knit into the front of the second stitch.

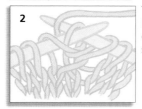

**2** Then knit into the back of the first stitch.

**3** Slip both stitches off the left needle together.

## • Right Twist Variations

To work a knit-and-purl right twist, knit into the front of the second stitch, then purl the first stitch. To twist two stitches to the right on a wrong-side row, purl into the front of the second stitch, then into the front of the first stitch.

## Herringbone Twist

Multiple of 6 sts plus 3.

This twist pattern uses left and right twists on a stockinette stitch background, but the top stitches of the twists are made more prominent by slipping them on wrong-side rows.

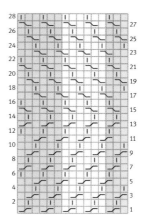

## Miniature Plait

Multiple of 4 sts plus 1.

Use this pattern as an interesting alternative to rib – simply plan more purl stitches between plaits to suit your design.

## Branched Rib

Multiple of 16 sts plus 2.

This decorated rib doesn't pull in very much, so can be used as an all-over pattern. If you want all the branches to twist in the same direction, repeat the first or last eight stitches of the chart.

## Bellflower Blocks

Multiple of 8 sts plus 6.

Simply twisting the stitches at the top of each block produces this pretty pattern.

P into front of 2nd st on left-hand needle, then in front of 1st st, sl both sts off needle tog.

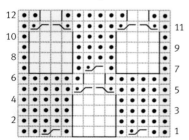

## Wave and Twist

Multiple of 14 sts plus 2.

Twist stitches are good for giving an Aran effect in miniature.

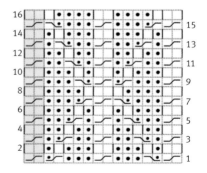

## Mock Cable

Multiple of 8 sts plus 1.

This attractive pattern is easier than it looks. It uses three-stitch twists.

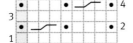

## Mock Cable 2

Multiple of 5 sts plus 2.

Simple twist stitches on the right side and purl rows on the wrong side make an easy stitch with plenty of texture.

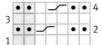

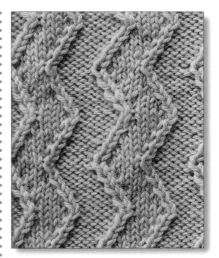

## Twisted Rib

Multiple of 4 sts plus 2.

Twisting together two stitches on every row makes a firm, well-defined rib.

(WS) P into front of 2nd st on left-hand needle, p into first st, sl both sts off needle tog.

## Zigzags

Multiple of 12 sts.

Stockinette stitch zigzags are outlined with twisted stitches for more definition and surface texture.

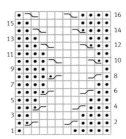

## Two-twist Lattice

Multiple of 8 sts plus 2.

For a three-twist lattice, simply work rows 1 and 2 twice, then rows 3–10. Work rows 11 and 12 twice, then rows 13–20, making a 24-row repeat. For a wider lattice, work on a multiple of 10 stitches, allowing two more purl stitches between twists on the first row, then moving the stitches four times to create the diamond shapes.

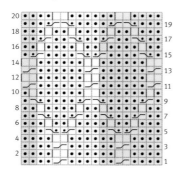

## Tiny Trellis

Multiple of 4 sts plus 2.

If worked over 10 stitches, this pattern makes a crossed diamond panel.

# Easy Twist Stitches

Twisting stitches is an easy way to create patterns where lines of stitches travel over the surface of the knitting.

## Easy Stitch 1

Multiple of 6 sts plus 3.

This stitch is reversible.

## Easy Stitch 2

Multiple of 7 sts.

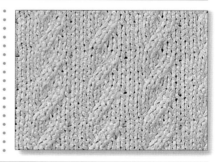

## Easy Stitch 3

Multiple of 4 sts plus 3.

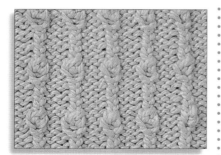

# Medium Twist Stitches

When the stitched patterns are densely twisted, it can make the fabric thicker and less flexible. To counteract this it is a good idea to use larger needles.

## Medium Stitch 2

Multiple of 9 sts plus 3.

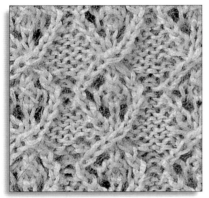

## Medium Stitch 1

Multiple of 8 sts plus 1.

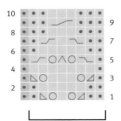

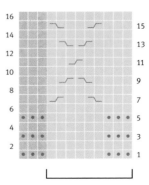

## Medium Stitch 3

Multiple of 8 sts plus 1.

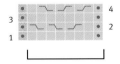

## Medium Stitch 4

Multiple of 5 sts plus 4.

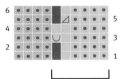

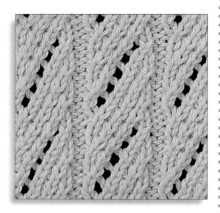

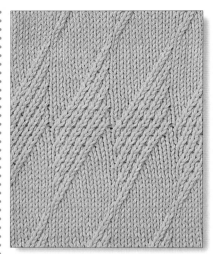

## Medium Stitch 5

## Medium Stitch 6

Multiple of 9 sts plus 2.

Multiple of 10 sts.

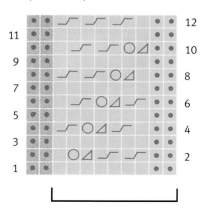

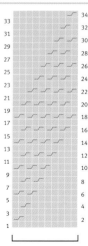

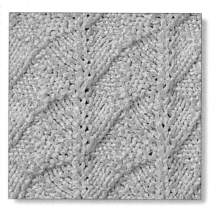

## Medium Stitch 7

## Medium Stitch 8

Multiple of 6 sts plus 2.

Multiple of 12 sts plus 1.

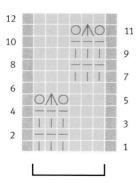

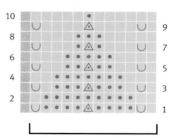

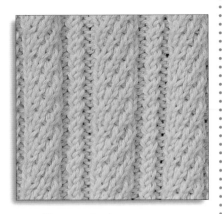

## Medium Stitch 9

Multiple of 12 sts plus 6.

## Medium Stitch 10

Multiple of 13 sts plus 7.

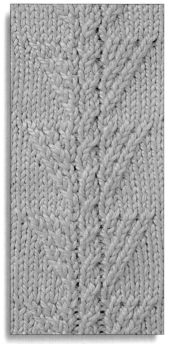

## Medium Stitch 11

Panel of 16 sts.

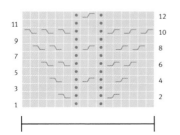

## Medium Stitch 12

Multiple of 10 sts.

(K1, p1, k1, p1, k1) in st to make 5 sts from 1.

K5 on RS rows, p5 on WS rows.

P5tog.

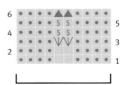

## Medium Stitch 13

Multiple of 8 sts plus 1.

Note that rows 9–16 are a multiple of 4 sts plus 5.

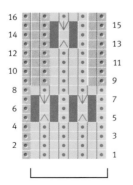

## Medium Stitch 14

Panel of 28 sts.

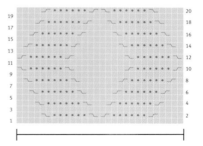

## Medium Stitch 15

Multiple of 10 sts plus 2.

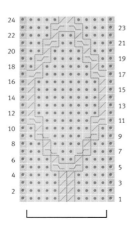

## Medium Stitch 16

Multiple of 9 sts plus 3.

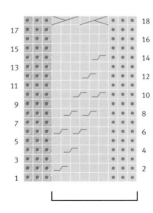

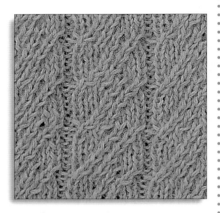

## Medium Stitch 17

Multiple of 10 sts plus 2.

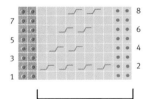

## Medium Stitch 18

Multiple of 10 sts plus 6.

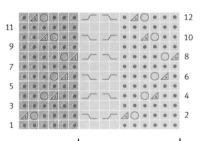

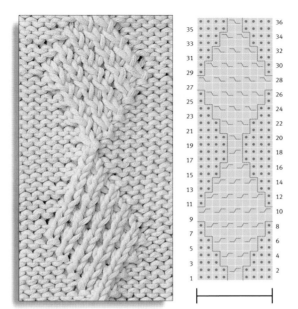

## Medium Stitch 19

Panel of 10 sts.

## Medium Stitch 20

Multiple of 16 sts plus 8.

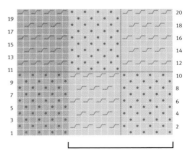

## Medium Stitch 21

Motif of 19 sts.

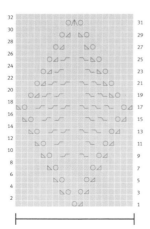

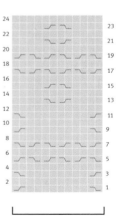

## Medium Stitch 22

Multiple of 12 sts.

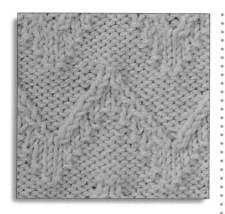

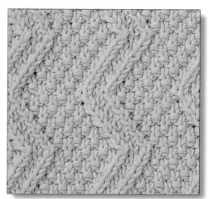

## Medium Stitch 23

Multiple of 12 sts.

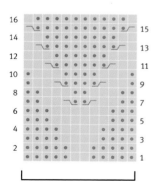

## Medium Stitch 24

Multiple of 12 sts plus 3.

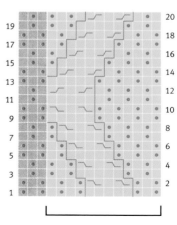

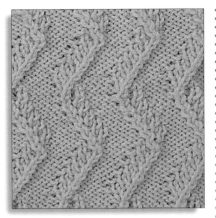

## Medium Stitch 25

Multiple of
9 sts.

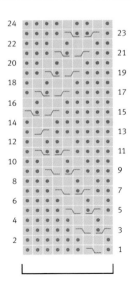

## Medium Stitch 26

Multiple of 15 sts plus 2.

(P1, k1, p1, k1, p1) in st to make 5 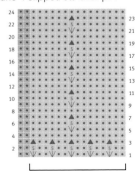 sts from 1.

K5.

With yarn at back, sl 4 sts purlwise, p1, take 4 slipped sts over p1.

# Difficult Twist Stitches

Twisting stitches is an easy way to create patterns where lines of stitches travel over the surface of the knitting. Some twist stitch patterns look like miniature cables, others create diagonals, zigzags, and diamonds. The patterns in this section can be quite a challenge to master, but the results are worth the effort.

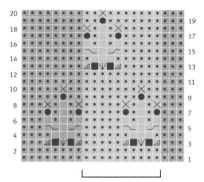

## Difficult Stitch 1

Multiple of 10 sts plus 11.

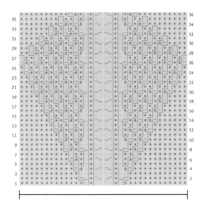

## Difficult Stitch 2

Panel of 11 sts.

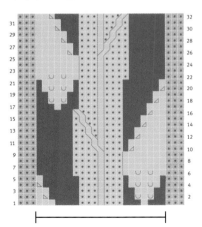

## Difficult Stitch 3

Motif of 34 sts.

## Difficult Stitch 4

Multiple of 10 sts plus 2.

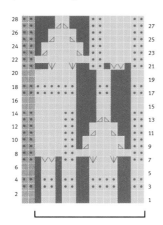

## Difficult Stitch 5

Panel of 17 sts.

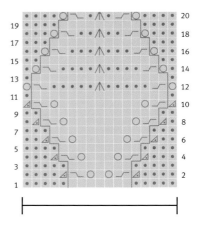

# Difficult Stitch 6

This fruit basket pattern is a stunning addition to your repertoire.

Chart A is worked first and is a motif of 54 sts, decreased to 53 sts on row 39. Chart B is then worked consecutively, the motif starting with 53 sts on row 41. The stitch count then varies until 53 sts are resumed on row 106.

## Chart A (Basket)

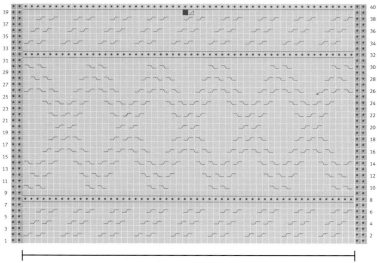

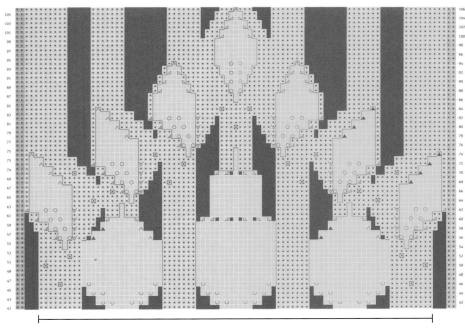

**Chart B (Fruit)**

## Difficult Stitch 7

Multiple of 28 sts plus 32.

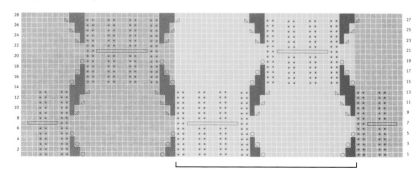

# Glossary

2-ply, 3-ply, 4-ply: Knitting with two colors in the same row.

Backstitch: A firm sewing stitch.

Binding off: Fastening off stitches so they do not unravel.

Block, blocking: Treating a piece of knitting to set its shape.

Bouclé yarn: A fancy yarn with a knobbly effect.

Button band or button border: A piece, knitted sideways or lengthwise, to which buttons are sewn.

Buttonhole band or buttonhole border: A piece, knitted sideways or lengthwise, with buttonholes worked as knitting proceeds.

Cable needle: A short, double-pointed knitting needle for working cables.

Cable: A group of stitches crossed over another group of stitches.

Casting on: Making new stitches on a needle.

Chunky: A heavy-weight yarn.

Circular needle: A long, double-pointed knitting needle with a flexible center section, used for working in the round, or working large numbers of stitches.

Cuff: The lower border of a sleeve.

Decreasing: Working stitches together to reduce their number.

Double-pointed needle: A knitting needle with a point at each end.

Duplicate stitch: Another name for swiss darning.

Dye lot number: Indicates the exact dye bath used to dye the yarn in question, not just the shade.

Ease: The difference between the body measurement and the measurement of a garment.

Eyelet: A small hole for a button or as part of a lace stitch pattern.

Fair Isle: Knitting with two colors in the same row.

Fingering: A fine-weight yarn (similar to 2-ply and 3-ply).

Float: The strand of yarn left at the wrong side of the work when stranding.

Fully-fashioned shaping: Shaping emphasized by working decreases (or increases) two or more stitches in from the edge of the work.

Garter stitch: Formed by working all stitches as knit on every row, or all stitches as purl on every row.

Gauge: The number of stitches and rows to a given measurement.

Hank: A coil of yarn.

Increasing: Making extra stitches.

Intarsia: The technique of "picture" knitting.

Knitwise: As when knitting a stitch.

Long stitch: A stitch made by wrapping the yarn twice around the needle.

Mattress stitch: The stitch used for the invisible seam.

Multiple: The number of stitches required for one pattern repeat.

Needle gauge: A small metal or plastic sheet with holes of different sizes, labeled with needle sizes, for checking the size of knitting needles.

Pattern repeat: The stitches and rows which must be repeated to form a stitch pattern.

Pattern: A stitch pattern or a set of instructions for making a garment.

Point protector: A plastic device to protect the point of a knitting needle.

Purlwise: As when purling a stitch.

Raglan: A sleeve and armhole shaping that slopes from the armhole to the neck edge.

Reverse stockinette stitch: Stockinette stitch worked with the purl side as the right side.

Rib stitches or ribbing: Various combinations of knit and purl stitches, arranged to form vertical lines.

Right and left (when describing parts of a garment): The terms that describe where the garment part will be when worn, e.g. the right sleeve is the sleeve worn on the right arm, not the sleeve on the right when the garment is viewed from the front.

Right side: The side of the work that will be the outside of the garment when worn.

Ring marker: A small split ring of metal or plastic, slipped onto a stitch or onto a needle to mark a particular position in the work.

Seam: The join made when two pieces of knitting are sewn together.

Seed stitch: A stitch pattern with a "dotted" appearance.

Selvage stitch: The first or last stitch of a row worked in a different way to the rest of the row, to make a decorative edge, or a firm, neat edge for seaming.

Set-in sleeve: A sleeve and armhole shaping where the armhole is curved to take a curved sleeve head.

Shaping: Increasing or decreasing the number of stitches to form the shape required.

Slip stitch: A stitch slipped from one needle to the other without working into it, or a simple sewing stitch taking one strand from one edge and one strand from the other.

Stitch holder: A device used for holding stitches temporarily.

Stockinette stitch: Formed by working one row of knit stitches, one row of purl stitches, and repeating these two rows.

Stranding: Carrying a color to a new position across the wrong side of the work.

Swiss darning: Embroidering over individual knitted stitches with another color.

Tapestry needle: A sewing needle with a blunt tip and a large eye.

Twist: A single stitch crossed over another stitch.

Twisting: Carrying a color across the wrong side of several stitches in another color, then twisting the two colors.

Worsted: A medium-weight yarn (similar to double knitting).

Wrong side: The side of the work that will be the inside of the garment when worn.

# Index

*A list of abbreviations can be found on page 96, followed by a glossary of symbols on pages 96 to 101.*

**WITHDRAWN**